Trim Carpentry
for the Homeowner

Glen Huey

BETTERWAY BOOKS
Cincinnati, Ohio
www.popularwoodworking.com

Read This Important Safety Notice

To prevent accidents, keep safety in mind while you work. Use the safety guards installed on power equipment; they are for your protection. When working on power equipment, keep fingers away from saw blades, wear safety goggles to prevent injuries from flying wood chips and sawdust, wear hearing protection and consider installing a dust vacuum to reduce the amount of airborne sawdust in your woodshop. Don't wear loose clothing, such as neckties or shirts with loose sleeves, or jewelry, such as rings, necklaces or bracelets, when working on power equipment. Tie back long hair to prevent it from getting caught in your equipment. People who are sensitive to certain chemicals should check the chemical content of any product before using it. The authors and editors who compiled this book have tried to make the contents as accurate and correct as possible. Plans, illustrations, photographs and text have been carefully checked. All instructions, plans and projects should be carefully read, studied and understood before beginning construction. Due to the variability of local conditions, construction materials, skill levels, etc., neither the author nor Betterway Books assumes any responsibility for any accidents, injuries, damages or other losses incurred resulting from the material presented in this book. Prices listed for supplies and equipment were current at the time of publication and are subject to change.

Metric Conversion Chart

to convert	to	multiply by
Inches	Centimeters	2.54
Centimeters	Inches	0.4
Feet	Centimeters	30.5
Centimeters	Feet	0.03
Yards	Meters	0.9
Meters	Yards	1.1

Trim Carpentry for the Homeowner. Copyright © 2008 by Glen Huey. Printed and bound in China. All rights reserved. No part of this book may be reproduced in any form or by any electronic or mechanical means including information storage and retrieval systems without permission in writing from the publisher, except by a reviewer, who may quote brief passages in a review. Published by Betterway Books, an imprint of F+W Publications, Inc., 4700 East Galbraith Road, Cincinnati, Ohio, 45236. First edition.

Distributed in Canada by Fraser Direct
100 Armstrong Avenue
Georgetown, Ontario L7G 5S4
Canada

Distributed in the U.K. and Europe by David & Charles
Brunel House
Newton Abbot
Devon TQ12 4PU
England
Tel: (+44) 1626 323200
Fax: (+44) 1626 323319
E-mail: postmaster@davidandcharles.co.uk

Distributed in Australia by Capricorn Link
P.O. Box 704
Windsor, NSW 2756
Australia

Visit our corporate Web site at www.fwpublications.com for information on more resources for home improvements and other how-to publications.

Other fine F+W Publications books are available from your local bookstore or direct from the publisher.

12   11   10   09   08   5   4   3   2   1

Library of Congress Cataloging-in-Publication Data

Huey, Glen, 1959-
  Trim carpentry for the homeowner / by Glen Huey.
    p. cm.
  Includes index.
  ISBN-10: 1-55870-814-6 (pbk. : alk. paper)
  ISBN-13: 978-1-55870-814-3 (pbk. : alk. paper)
  1. Trim carpentry--Amateurs' manuals. I. Popular woodworking. II. Title.
  TH5695.H845 2008
  694'.6--dc22   2007034910

Acquisitions editor: David Thiel
Senior editor: Jim Stack
Designer: Terri Woesner
Production coordinator: Mark Griffin
Photographer: Glen Huey
Illustrator: Len Churchill

fw
F+W PUBLICATIONS, INC.

About the Author

Glen grew up in the homebuilding business. His father had a successful building and real estate business for most of Glen's childhood. In fact, after graduating from the University of Cincinnati with a degree in business, and not landing a job dealing in stocks and bonds, Glen pulled his father out of retirement to start his own homebuilding business.

His early resume, in addition to homebuilder, includes construction superintendent and carpenter. Later, Glen decided to change professions and build furniture in a temperature controlled shop, instead of homes in the cold Ohio winter months.

As a furniture maker he has authored three books: *Fine Furniture for a Lifetime, Building Fine Furniture* and *Illustrated Guide to Building Period Furniture*, published by *Popular Woodworking* books.

In 2006 Glen joined the staff of *Popular Woodworking* magazine as a senior editor. While his passion is building and writing about furniture, he still considers himself a carpenter. Whether building furniture or building homes, it's the creative process that he craves.

Acknowledgements

Many thanks to the companies that helped me gather information and photos to fill this book.

Thanks to Great Traditions Homes in Cincinnati, Ohio and their sales manager, Chip Browne. Chip was my first contact that opened a model home for me to take photos.

Thanks to McCabe Lumber in Loveland, Ohio. Their showroom is full of doors, mouldings and mantles. They did not hesitate to allow me access to any area in the showroom (which is attached to the adjacent lumberyard where the products are available for immediate use). Inside the showroom they have a complete home that's full of finished carpentry that shows what is possible.

Thanks to One Stop Tool Rental in West Chester, Ohio. They graciously allowed me to take photos of floor refinishing tools. They were helpful and are knowledgeable about other tools you might need for general home repair.

Thanks to McSwain Carpet and Flooring in West Chester, Ohio. They allowed me to learn about and photograph hardwood flooring of all designs. The staff is knowledgeable about their products and eager to help.

Thanks also to David Thiel and Jim Stack of *Betterway Books*. I agreed to write this book at the same time that I joined the staff at *Popular Woodworking* magazine. My time on this book became short and my work slow. These guys found a way to extend me the time to pull things together.

contents

Introduction

After a career in the world of education, my grandfather worked as a carpenter and painter. My father was in the homebuilding business for more than 30 years. As a result, my background is extensive when dealing with projects around the house. My wife is amazed at the things I consider do-it-yourself jobs.

I spent several years working with my father in the homebuilding business. Later, I started my own homebuilding company. I eventually left that career to build reproduction furniture. Then, a few years later, I joined the staff of *Popular Woodworking* magazine. When I sat down to write this book, each of the homebuilding tips and techniques that I had learned easily came back to me.

As you peruse the pages of this book and learn the techniques, you'll notice that the methods I use are dated. I like tried-and-trued methods that have stood the test of time and are passed from generation to generation.

Because your home is possibly your most valuable asset, it should be properly cared for and maintained. If you choose to replace a door, fix kitchen cabinets or build a windowseat, you want the construction or repair to last. You don't want to leave it in disrepair. It takes a few short hours on the weekend to do the necessary upkeep and to add features. You may have a neighbor ask for your advice or become the go-to person for home repair in your neighborhood.

If you are in the business of remodeling homes (sometimes called *flipping*) you need to do the job right. Nothing is as hard to build or as easy to lose as a reputation. By doing repairs the right way, you'll be able to maintain and build on a good reputation. Now days, home buyers are well read and knowledgeable. All it takes is one small error and the sale — along with your reputation — is gone.

In the pages of this book you'll find ways to quickly fix a door that sags or, change a rough opening hang a replacement door in its stead. You'll also discover short, inexpensive fixes that may save you a major repair.

As you look at the list of tools for doing trim carpentry work around your home, rental property or properties that you're renovating, don't become overwhelmed.

tools
and materials

Upon first inspection the list appears enormous. But, if you dig

into the tools you may find that a large number of them are already

around the house. Many of these tools are part of any household

inventory. And, if you enjoy doing odd jobs around the house, there

may be only a few items on the list that you don't own. If some of

This is a good, basic miter box and saw. You can cut
45° miters all day long with it.

these tools haven't yet found their way into your
toolbox, please don't go out and buy the entire
list all at once. There's no need to purchase tools
unless you have a specific need for them. Because
each aspect of trim carpentry requires different
tools, I recommend that you buy the tools as you
need them.

For instance, if you need to reattach a loose
piece of door casing you don't need to buy an air
compressor and nail gun. A hammer, nail set and a
few finish nails are enough to complete this task.

If, on the other hand, you plan to create wainscot by using a series of different mouldings (see

chapter seven), purchasing a miter saw and that air
compressor with a nail gun is a smart move.

Look at the different design ideas throughout
this book. When you decide what items would add
the most value to your home, read through the
steps and plan your work. This method helps you
edit the list of tools down to what you need. The
money you save by not buying unnecessary tools
can be put towards additional renovation.

The tools listed are by no means in order of
importance. The only grouping I've done is to
arrange similar tools together. We'll look at saws,
tools for measuring, air-powered tools and their

A compound sliding miter saw is a good choice for cutting mouldings, narrow or wide.

accessories, screws and hardware, paint supplies and other miscellaneous tools that you'll find helpful if not necessary.

Hand, Power and Specialty Saws

Trim carpentry is all about the installation of mouldings — lots of mouldings. And one of the most useful tools for installing those mouldings is a **miter saw**. Miter saws are available in a myriad of selections. From the $20 **hand miter saw**,

which is basically a miter box that is fabricated from plastic or wood with a mating saw to the **sliding compound miter saw** has a head that tilts from side to side and travels forward and backward. This saw can make cuts over 11" in width when set at 90°.

Which do you choose? You have to look at the type and amount of work you're planning to find an answer. I always look at the inexpensive end of the spectrum, buy somewhere in the middle of the pack and hope for the best, (unless the more expensive tool is the better value for the work I'm doing).

A low-end **miter saw** is only good for cutting a handful of mouldings. After you make a number of

A basic miter saw (chop saw) is a good middle-of-the-road choice for the majority of miter cuts you'll ever need to make.

cuts with a **plastic miter box** your arms are tired and your nerves are shot and you realize that accuracy in the cut is hard to find. Don't skimp on the miter saw.

Of course, on the opposite end of the spectrum there is the top-of-the-line **sliding compound miter saw**. At a cost of $400 - $600 this can be a sweet investment or an unnecessary expenditure depending on how much cutting you do.

My recommendation is to buy something in the middle. Look for a **miter saw** that cuts 45° angles when positioned to the right or left of 90° (some-

times referred to as a **chop saw**). In my opinion, tilting the head (on a **compound miter saw**) is only necessary if you plan to install crown moulding the hard way, using compound angle cuts. This is something I avoid if possible. (Chapter five explains the easy method for cutting crown moulding.) You should choose a 10" or 12" blade since a smaller blade reduces the width of the cut. And please, stick with a known brand name.

Jigsaws are another valuable tool to have when doing trim work. A **jigsaw** can perform a wide variety of tasks and can substitute for other

A jigsaw is a versitile tool that can be used to cut straight and curved lines. The base plate can be tilted for making bevel cuts.

A coping saw is a good tool to use for removing material for, oddly enough, coped moulding joints.

Choose a wide measuring tape that will support itself when extended to at least five feet.

tools. Think about ripping material. If you don't have a table saw (an unnecessary expenditure in trim carpentry) you can use a **jigsaw** to make rip cuts. You could also use a **circular saw**. But, you have more control with the **jigsaw**. And notched cuts, those two-step cuts sometimes used at the ends of a window stool, are much easier with a hand-held **jigsaw**. With a bi-metal blade you can even use the saw for cutting stubborn nails that refuse to release their hold. It is worth spending the money necessary to purchase a good mid-spectrum **jigsaw**.

The **coping saw** is a specialized tool. There is only one use for this tool that makes sense. Cutting the waste material from mouldings to allow that perfect, coped fit (see chapter five). This saw allows you to move, twist and turn in any direction to complete the cut. The blades are thin, flexible and can break easily. Buy a pack of blades because you'll wind up needing a few, especially if you haven't used this saw before. But once you master the saw (or at least understand how it works) it is most useful. At under $15 any **coping saw** is a good choice.

The combination square is versitile. It can be used to check for 45° and 90° angles, set to a particular measurement and, if the head is removed, a ruler or straightedge.

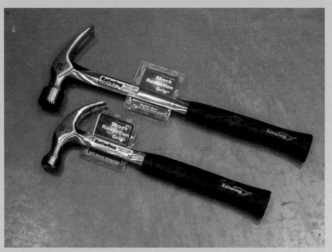

A framing hammer (upper) has fairly straight claws that can be used as a pry bar. The finish hammer (lower) is lighter and the claws are curved for ease in pulling nails.

Tools for Making Measurements

Measuring is second only to cutting in trim carpentry. Without accurate measurements your job could be a fiasco. Don't try to save money on your **tape measure**, **level** or **combination square**. A penny saved here could add immensely to your aggravation factor later.

When deciding on a **measuring tape** look for one that is either 12'- or 16'-long with a locking mechanism that is above the tape. The tape itself should be ³/4" wide and the end should be a plate that's riveted for increased durability — even so, don't let the tape snap back into the case as it returns, it reduces longevity. The end is riveted and moves slightly to compensate for the thickness of the end of the catch. It's supposed to do that. Also, the markings or measurement indicators should be easy to read and printed on both edges of the tape.

If you want to find out if a line is parallel to the floor or if a door jamb is plum (vertical), you need a **level**. A **level** has bubbles incased in small glass tubes. Those bubbles indicate a true level or plumb line when the bubbles settle between the lines etched on the glass tubes. Your level should be a minimum of 24" in length, but 48" is better for installing windows and doors. The American standard is an **I-beam level**. In Europe the **box-beam level** is used regularly. Either will do the job required, but the **I-beam** is cheaper.

A **combination square** might be the least known of the recommended measuring tools. It's used for general squaring of materials and for laying out reveals when installing casing at the doors or windows. Look for a 12" tool that slides easily and holds its position when locked. You can find bargains when searching for this tool, but make sure the markings are clear and correct and stay away from metric measurements unless that is the unit with which you work.

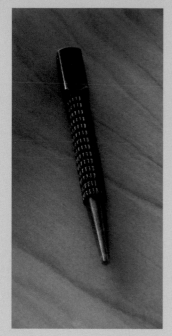

Nail sets come in assorted sizes — $1/32"$, $2/32"$ and $3/32"$ being the most common.

A waffle-head hammer is a heavy framing hammer. The textured head keeps the hammer from slipping off nail heads when in use. The marks left are of no consequence when doing rough framing but it's not used for finish work.

Hammers, Muscle and Air-Powered

When nailing trim moulding in place you must decide whether to complete the job by hand or gain an edge by using a nail gun. When you look at the initial expenditure, one is very economical and the other is more costly. But that's only half the story. If time means anything to you the second scenario might just be a better value.

A standard **hammer** will set you back about $20 - $40. If you determine it's best to purchase the **air-powered gun**, you should still have a **hammer** in your arsenal. And, you need a **nail set** as well. (You might already have one in the handyman drawer at the house.) If you don't here's what to look for.

The biggest consideration on a **hammer** is the weight — which is measured in ounces. Most hammers are 16 - 28 ounces in weight. The light ham-

mers are for finish work while the heavy hammers are for framing work. Look for a light to medium weight to do most jobs around the house. Also, don't buy any **special headed hammers**. **Waffle head hammers** look great and powerful, but miss a nail and ding the trim, and, you're created a repair for yourself. Not so cool.

Another important feature in hammers is the **claw** — the rear portion that allows you to pull nails. This should be anywhere from **straight to slightly curved**. If you select a hammer with a highly curved claw you'll find places that nail pulling is restricted because you cannot get the hammer into position to grab the nail. The handle restricts the process because of the angle needed to grab the nail. Don't get hung up on a **wooden handle** versus a **fiberglass handle**. That hammer is going to outlive you if it's used properly. Either handle is fine.

Driving nails with a hammer takes skill, and there are times when you have to drill a hole prior to driving the nail, usually when you are close to an edge or in hardwood. You also have to use the **nail set** to pound the nails below the moulding's surface to allow filler to do its job. To eliminate those extra steps and to speed the process along, you might want to turn to an **air-powered nail gun** and a **compressor**.

You will need a **compressor** to operate a **nail gun** or, depending on the size of the nail, a **brad gun**. **Nail guns** shoot a 16-gauge nail up to 2½" in length while most **brad guns** use an 18-gauge brad that is up to 2" in length. The cost for both is sometimes a bit high. Expect to pay $200 - $400 for

a complete kit, including an **air compressor**. As with the **miter saw**, you need to think about how often you will use a nail gun to determine if this is the right purchase.

There are several **nail gun** manufacturers. Their tools are similar with minor variances in design and in the size nails each gun can shoot. A **brad gun** will suffice for most work in trim carpentry, but if you plan to install new walls or do a large amount of heavy remodeling, add a nailer to your cache.

Don't forget to include nails with whatever nail driving device you choose. For hand-hammering include some 3d ($1^1/4$"), 6d (2") and 8d ($2^1/2$") finish nails. It doesn't hurt to have a few common nails on hand too. Common nails have heads that are set flat to the surface while finish nails have minuscule heads that are driven below the surface.

Be sure the nails fit your particular gun, or match the nail gauge to the gun's capabilities. A 16-gauge nail won't work in the 18-gauge brad gun.

Also, consider the amount of nails you purchase. Some makers are packaging nails for air-powered tools in smaller quantities. If you cannot find smaller boxes, you'll end up spending more cash.

Drills, Drill Bits and Screws

When I was doing trim carpentry I had both **battery** and **electric drills**. Invariably the battery drill would quit just as I reached a major need for it. I would then turn to the electric to finish the job while the battery drill recharged.

It is most important to have a **battery powered drill**. Having the backup electric drill is no longer so important because most suppliers sell kits that include two **batteries**, a **charger** and the drill, so one battery is always on the charger. With recharge times as short as thirty minutes, there is seldom a time when you won't have a fully-charged battery.

Battery-powered drills have proven to be invaluable to carpenters, woodworkers and for around-the-house use — drilling holes, installing screws and stirring paint.

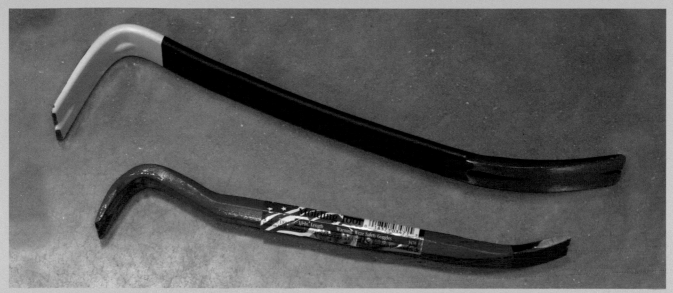

Pry bars come in a variety of sizes and are good for, of course, prying — but also for removing nails and, when dropped, scaring your cat.

A very sturdy chisel and a low-angle (the blade angle is almost flat in the plane) block plane. The low-angle blade cuts easily and cleanly.

The most important part of the drill kit is the **battery**. Lithium-Ion batteries, the newest technology, are far better than the older nickel-cadmium batteries because they are more powerful and have a longer run time. Plus, they last nearly four times longer. And with Lithium-Ion batteries you don't have the "slow death" as you did with the nickel-cadmium batteries. The Lithium-Ion batteries hold constant power until the juice is gone. Look for the newer batteries if you're buying a kit and settle for no less than an 18-volt unit. That's enough power to get through most jobs with ease.

An accoutrement of accessories to go along with the drills includes a **magnetic bit tip holder** and a selection of different bit tips. (Chances are you'll work mainly with **Phillips screwdriver** tips, but you should be aware of different tips such as the square drive.) The screw sizes are varied. I suggest buying them as you need them and warehousing any extras after the job is complete. Also, it's smart to have a **set of drill bits** on hand. A pack of five or six good quality bits is far better than buying a package of thirty bits, of which only a few sizes are worth owning and using.

Miscellaneous Extras

Here's a laundry list of extra items needed for doing trim work around the house. Pick up a bundle of **wood shims** if you're doing work around a door or window frame. As mentioned before, a nail set should be added to the cart as should a **utility knife, pry bar** and **goggles**. Pick up a **chalk line** for snapping straight lines along walls. Of course, a few **pencils** are a great addition too.

You may also want a chisel or two and a block plane. The chisels assume many jobs, but the block plane has a specific duty and should be treated with care.

Purchase a set of low-end **chisels**. I mean no disrespect when I use the term *low-end*. Chisels can be extremely expensive or rather cheap. There are numerous uses for chisels in trim carpentry and they can be hard on the tools. (I remember using my chisel as a pry bar once.) Look for a sturdy handle with a metal cap on the end. Chances are you'll be tapping that cap with your hammer, not a wooden mallet.

The **block plane** is used for trimming or fine-tuning moulding cuts. I like a **low-angle block plane** for most jobs. Keep the blade sharp and try to limit the plane's uses to that one type of work.

Applying the Finish

The last step in most trim carpentry jobs is the finish. That's paint and stain we're talking about. The list for this work includes **paint brushes, paint rollers** and a **paint tray** or **pan**. A **paint edger** is indispensable when painting walls. (Look for more information about this tool in chapter ten). Also, a **putty knife, staining rags** and a **caulking gun** are good additions. And, the caulking gun won't be useful without caulk. A decent caulking gun is handy to have around and putty knives are inexpensive. I have two or three lying around my shop. And who can't find a million uses for rags? I use them to stain and clean up finishes.

I don't get bogged down in the paint area too much. A **good brush** does a good job while an inexpensive brush does not. Depending on the project and type of paint you're working with, buy a good brush. It's not the place to save a penny. If you're slapping paint on the wall corner for the roller to cover as you paint the walls, an inexpensive brush works fine. But try to use that brush for

A 2" or 2^{1}/$_{2}$" china bristle brush are good brushes. Keep them clean and they last a long time. I like an angle tip for fine work and a flat tip for everything else.

Buy an inexpensive metal pan, then use a pan cover. When done painting and the job is finished, the pan covers are thrown away.

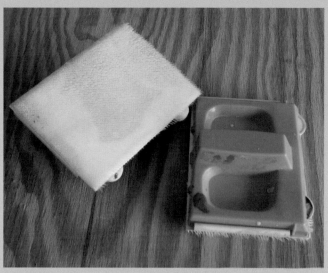

The paint edger is a must for painting walls. You can use it to paint into corners, around door and window trim and baseboards.

detail painting around the window and you're asking for trouble. To me a good brush is a 2" or 2½" china bristle brush. Keep it clean and it lasts a long time. I like an angle tip for fine work and a flat tip for everything else.

As for the balance of the painting supplies I choose to go inexpensive (I'll get into more detail in chapter ten). I sacrifice when it comes to the paint roller though. It's best not to buy the cheapest one available since this tool will be used repeatedly. As for **roller covers**, I like to roll paint onto the walls, then throw the used roller into the garbage when the job is done. Time spent cleaning a roller cover is time wasted. I feel the same about roller trays or pans. I buy a cheap metal **paint pan** and then I use a **pan cover** that sets me back a buck. When the job is finished, off to the trash the cover goes. Time is valuable.

These are the tools that I found most useful for all the trim work I do around my house. Again, evaluate your job. There is no need to purchase all these tools at once. You may never need a nail or brad gun and compressor or a pry bar, but if you do, this is a good list of the tools to refer to.

flip tip

As a do-it-yourself homeowner, you probably have the tools needed to get started doing some basic trim carpentry work. Check your toolboxes, drawers and shelves in your garage, in your basement and in your house. Roundup all the tools and take inventory of what you have before buying any new tools.

2

Searching for design ideas is a daunting task, especially when you have to start making those decisions. If you're under pressure, these tasks become harder by

design
ideas

the minute. So, you have to be ready when the time presents itself.

That translates into being prepared. Hey, we prepare for a lot of

things in our lives, and renovating our homes by adding trim and

changing mouldings is something that fits into that category.

But how do you prepare for a project like this? Turn to your resources. I find local showrooms the best source of inspiration and aid for those renovating decisions. Home centers and the local lumber company's showrooms provide handsomely by having the products for you to hold and see when working on a design scheme. Also, some larger homebuilders have showrooms that feature the products they use in their homes.

Another area that I find most helpful in obtaining design ideas is magazines. The number of magazines published monthly or yearly that have design topics as their primary agenda is staggering. But, it doesn't have to be a magazine devoted to design.

Also, turn to television shows. We watch too many hours of TV, according to some, so why not make it work for us by learning design ideas, small

project methods and what products are available to work with?

How about local home shows? The local board of realtors in many areas has shows where homebuilders build a model home that is open to the public for a few weeks prior to either selling the home or allowing the purchaser to take possession of the place. These are great offerings when looking for an updated design or finding what the newest products are for sprucing up your abode.

Finally, take a look at Web sites. Many sites are dedicated to design and home decoration. While they have a few difficulties to overcome, they are certainly one of many avenues to walk down in the search for your design ideas.

Showrooms of the Suppliers

Some of us live close to *big-box* stores. They are great places to find products and inspiration for renovation. While these stores have a nice standard selection of items, they are somewhat limited in their total number of moulding profiles and major items you might need. Take door selections for example. I found a few designs that are common to everyday home use, but I wanted a special door design and it was nowhere to be found. Only items that the masses look for can be found at home centers. Don't forget, we're trying to add a personal touch to our homes. How can we do that if we find and use the same materials?

As I began to search for ideas that would change my home décor, I found the local lumberyard to be the place to start. I am comfortable in that environment; I grew up there. You should become acquainted with them as well.

A good lumberyard — look for one that supplies builders in your area with trim mouldings, doors and windows — has many special items. There's nothing better than having the pieces of moulding in your hand or being able to arrange the

Homearamas and openhouse tours are a great way to see and feel a wide range of design ideas.

different profiles in a stacked design to develop a moulding profile that is all yours. Take some time to see what profiles of casing match with a baseboard that's caught your eye. Look at the difference between ranch casing and traditional casing.

Try standing next to doors that are installed correctly and feeling the texture of the door as well as the doorknob as you open and close the unit. See the difference between a standard 6'8" door and a door that stands nearly 8' tall. Certainly you can see how this can influence your design ideas.

This is also a great opportunity to look into whether you want to paint your trim or use a stained finish, decide if you want to increase the budget to use a specific hardwood for your trim package or look into having a custom moulding

profile created that meets your specific design. All of these options are available at your local lumberyard. Look around. I'll bet you can find a great store near your home. The ideas abound. Make creative use of them.

Builders Showrooms

Some of the larger homebuilders have showrooms that are designed by professionals. These locations are there for home buyers to visit and make decisions about wallpaper, kitchen cabinets and fireplace surrounds for their newly purchased and soon-to-be-built homes.

They're also there to influence potential buyers to make the leap, so they have a nice selection of

Some stores feature a variety of mouldings from which to choose.

different aspects of home design. Also, there are many designs that use combinations of mouldings, ideas for nooks or niches that might fit perfectly into your décor. How about using a conventional item in a new way such as louvered shutters as a kitchen design element?

Stop by one of these showrooms for a look at room settings that allow you to see the items in use. There are not as many potential products, but viewing them in their environment has its benefits.

Design by Magazine

I know you've spent hours reading magazines. Most of us have. We pay close attention to the item we're trying to learn about, but do we notice the rooms in which that item is set? Not usually.

I advertised for a number of years in *Early American Life* magazine as I built a career in mak-

ing reproduction furniture. I always looked at the advertisements, mine as well as my competitor's. Seldom did I look at the rooms in the articles. When I decided to write this book, I went back and spent time studying those rooms and was amazed at what I saw. There were so many design ideas. I noticed mouldings, both crown and baseboard, that looked great. I saw rooms full of paneled walls — they ranged from chair rail height to full walls. Thumbing through the pages, I came upon a room that was a fully paneled library and immediately started planning to install something like it in my own home. I wondered if I missed this in all the magazines I had delivered to my house!

Today, you don't necessarily need to look at magazines that you've bought. There are lots of magazines dedicated to interior design, like *Traditional Home, Country Living, Metropolitan Living,* and *House Beautiful,* to name a few. Each issue is loaded with design ideas. All you need to do is figure out how the mouldings are arranged to achieve the look you want for your home. Style is left out. It's possible to see Shaker and Contemporary designs within the pages of one magazine and the American Federal period alongside a Country design that's painted in bright, vibrant colors in another.

Nothing is going to make a potential buyer or guest at your home take notice more than to seeing a design that appears to have leaped from the pages of a prominent magazine. Not only are they going to be moved (maybe so much as to make an offer to buy or spread the word around the neighborhood about your design ideas), they are also going to feel as comfortable in your home as you.

A Lazy Way to Design

Americans watch too much television. You hear it reported somewhere on the news at least weekly. Funny thing is, if we weren't watching television,

Magazines are a wonderful and rich resource for design ideas, room arrangements, window styles, door styles, flooring, etc.

Last, but by no means least, let's not forget the design idea program that may have started it all — the ever-popular public television station's *This Old House*. I think this show was the first one that sold people on rebuilding homes and taught them how to go about the work without trepidation. Watching this show made anyone that was remotely interested in fixing a home anxious to begin the process, whether they wanted to sell for a profit or simply wanted to enjoy living in it for years. Today the show continues along that same path, urging us to take on a renovation project.

we would not have seen the news. Still, television is an excellent medium for design ideas.

Who doesn't remember the show Dallas? Each week we watched J.R. walk into Southfork ranch after some dastardly oil business deal. Did any of us notice the wall coverings or the mouldings that lined the entry hall? Did you see the fireplace and how the wood wrapped the firebox in a raised panel design?

It's even easier to find design ideas on the television today. Cable or satellite television has brought us specialty channels. Two big stations are *HGTV (Home and Garden Television)* and *TLC (The Learning Channel)*. And there are others, both large and small, that give design advice daily.

Many of these shows are about older homes that people have updated. You see how the homes were when they were built and after they've been remodeled. Shows such as *Flip This House* and *Design on a Dime* show you design ideas and explain in detail the work that is done. This can help you decide which projects you can accomplish with a little carpentry background and which ones require a professional. Is there any better information than this?

Enjoy a Home Show, But Take Notes

When the idea came about to have homes built to showcase builders, designers and subcontractors, I was a small fry. In my area these showcases started in the 1960s. Back then my father participated in *Homearama*, where a group of homebuilders purchased building lots on one street, built homes, then charged people a small fee to come into the area and view the homes.

The homebuilders were hoping they could sell a few of these homes or other homes that were to be built. As a customer, you had a home ready to move into after the show dates were complete, or you had a chance to see how rooms and houses could be arranged by some of the area's top designers.

Travel forward some 40 years, and today the same shows are being held around the country. In our area, we have shows sponsored by homebuilding associations and even by local counties. What better place to stroll through homes that are designed by the brightest, most influential designers around and gather ideas that you can bring back to your home?

If you're looking to update your home or to turn houses for a profit, you should visit these events.

Some showrooms have large displays of just about any moulding profile and door and window hardware that is available. They will sometimes allow you to have small cut off pieces to work with when creating your own designs.

Ideas abound, but remember to bring a notebook. You'll see so many fresh looks that you'll lose track and be lucky to recall more than a few, once you're back inside your own four walls.

Online Design

Finally, there's the Internet. This global shopping center and design emporium is filled with Web sites for every aspect of home design. If you cannot find a moulding that fits into a specific room or stack-moulding profile, it's probably not being made (or maybe there's a small business enterprise to check into).

There are many sites with this type of information and it can be overwhelming. There are Web sites for laying out or arranging furniture, sites for replacement windows and specialty doors, numer-

ous sites that show wainscot and paneling and a few that deal in how-to themes.

The sky is certainly the limit when the internet is involved. But, you'll notice that I listed this last in the design ideas section. As I stated above, I think this is too much information. If you start searching without a plan, without first looking at a different source for ideas, it's very easy to get bogged down and not reach any decisions about renovating. Having an understanding of what you're searching for in the first place will make the internet a useful source of information.

3

In my opinion, windows are designed to be viewed from the outside looking in. Invariably we hang curtains and blinds that cover the insides of most windows.

window
trim and casings

But, occasionally they are seen. With that in mind,

they need to look good, no matter what window styles are pres-

ent in the house. And style is a personal choice. I'm partial to

double-hung, divided-light windows. I like the look. You may like

the look or usefulness of sliders or casement windows — those

windows that swing like doors.

WINDOW OPTIONS

 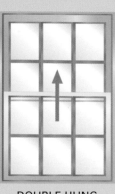   

PICTURE
(non-operable) DOUBLE HUNG CASEMENT AWNING ROLLING/SLIDING

3-1

A window wrapped in drywall is plain looking. Adding a sill, apron and trim will add appreciably to the look.

Looking Good

What makes a window look good? First, the glass needs to be free from breakage. If it's insulated glass (and I hope it is with today's energy prices) there should be no haze or cloudiness between the panes (see how to repair windows in chapter nine). But ultimately it's the trim mouldings around the windows that draw attention and adulation.

You don't have any wood mouldings around your windows? When installed, they can significantly raise the value of your home. The mouldings are going to give your property the edge when you're looking for a tenant or for someone to purchase your dwelling.

Years ago, installing windows and wrapping the drywall back to the unit was the favored method. At that time, vinyl-clad metal windows were the design, whether the style was single-hung, double-hung or casement. Then using wood windows became popular — because we studied and understood the concept of heat loss. Today, on homes at the middle and lower end of the pricing structure, homebuilders are again using drywall to wrap the windows. The drywall is less expensive, but I suggest casing your window in your home with wood trim (Photo 3-1).

Changing or adding casing to a window is like changing or adding casing on doors. You add a new design by using a wider standard casing, adding special features such as plinth blocks (even carved plinth blocks), or jazzing up the pieces of the casing with different types of profiles.

Getting Started

If you have windows in which the drywall is simply returned to the frame, you have the most work ahead of you (Photo 3-2). There are a few methods to choose from.

3-2

3-3

JAMB EXTENDER

3-4

Windows are generally cased in one of two ways. Some windows are cased as a picture frame — meaning that all four sides of the unit are cased identical. Others are finished by installing a sill (or stool), and an apron as a bottom edge treatment. The rest of the window is wrapped with casing.

Chances are that some type of stool is in place when the drywall is wrapped to the window (Photo 3-3). Marble sills used to be common, but today we're seeing more wooden sills. That sill has to be pulled out and replaced. It's not going to be wide enough to extend past any added mouldings. Insert a piece of wood that can be painted to match the mouldings. (You'll have to caulk the wood/drywall joint to make it disappear.)

Remember that you get what you pay for, but you can treat your humdrum windows by simply adding the mouldings to the wall face and not working with the drywall returns at all. Be sure to paint everything if this is the approach you take. Staining the wood trim and positioning it to a drywall return will look terrible.

A good solution is to add jamb extenders, which are pieces of wood cut to fit tight to the window frame and flush with the wall finish. They can be as thin as 1/4", but 3/4" is better (Photo 3-4).

If there's room to fit the extenders to the window without removing the wrapped drywall you're in good shape. If there isn't enough room, then you need to remove the drywall. At this point, the project just got more involved. I would consider your options carefully.

When you add the casing around the opening at the end, you should have a good amount of coverage at the wall. Start removing the drywall about an inch from the corner or just past any corner bead (the metal or plastic corners used in drywall work). At that range, you can easily cover any raw edges with mouldings.

3-5

Installing Jamb Extenders

1/4"-thick jamb extenders have to be nailed to the drywall and to any gaps caulked full prior to painting. There's not enough strength to keep the sides straight when using material of that thickness. I suggest that the extenders be made 3/4"-thick.

To begin proper installation of the extenders for either casing method, assemble the pieces into a box-like unit, slide it into position and attached to the wall while it is inset tight to the window. Use wooden shims to lock the unit in place, then nail through the extender structure into the wall studs or materials framing the window. Nailing the corners of the box tightly shows a good fit and allows for either a painted or a stained finish. Once

the extender is nailed in place you're ready to add the trim mouldings to complete the job.

Preparing for New Mouldings

If you didn't have to add the jamb extenders because your windows have trim already in place, and you want to change the trim moulding to add to the overall design, you need to strip the existing mouldings from the window.

This job needs to be approached with care for both doors and windows. If you damage the walls while removing any trim, you'll add to your expense (Photo 3-5).

Cut any caulking with a utility knife and use a wooden shim as a backing for the pry bar as you

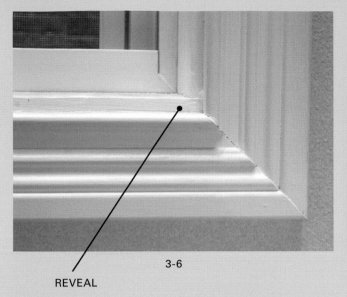

3-6

REVEAL

3-7

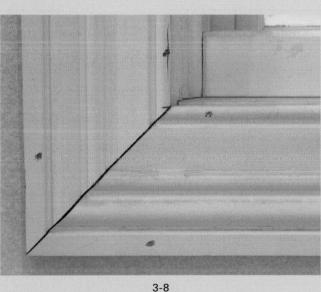

3-8

remove existing pieces. Begin at the top by working the moulding free, then work down each leg of the frame, carefully popping the trim away from the wall.

If you're removing an existing sill or stool, check to see how the sill is fitted to the window. Some windows have a small spacer that is easily stripped from the unit as you pull the sill and apron. Once the old mouldings are pulled from the window, it's time to add the new look.

Picture Frame Design

This is the easiest trim design to add to your windows. It's like making a picture frame. Begin with the bottom piece and cut a 45° angle at one end. Position that piece at the window leaving a 1/4" reveal and mark the opposite end also so there's a 1/4" reveal. (The reveal is a small flat portion of the window or jamb extender. Photo 3-6.)

This flat surface does two things for the design. First it adds another shadow line to the look. Second, it allows room for adjustment.

Fit the bottom piece of trim in place and nail it to both the wall and the window or jamb extender. Use 2" nails at the wall and 3/4" nails at the window.

Install the two vertical pieces of trim. Cut the ends at 45° and match one end of each piece with the cut ends of the bottom piece.

The final piece to the puzzle is the top one. It's also the hardest piece to fit because it needs to match up with the existing 45° cuts of the side pieces with both corners fit at the same time.

If all the pieces are cut accurately and are installed square to the window, you should be able to fit the top easily. To do so, cut the angle on one end then invert the piece at the window, matching the point of the top piece with that of the vertical piece. With the points matched exactly, mark the intersection of the other end to the upright point of the side casing. This is the exact length to cut the top piece. Make the cut and check the fit. It's sometimes necessary to fuss with the angles to achieve a better fit. This should be done with a low-angle block plane. (Photo 3-7.)

This is where a painted trim is more forgiving than that of a stained finish. With paint you can caulk any small gaps, cracks or crevices and the paint will cover. On a stained finish the fit must be tighter because fillers stand out and are very noticeable. (Photo 3-8.)

Trimming with a Sill and Apron

This is the showiest treatment of window casing. Yes, you can take it up a notch by using special mouldings and those glitzy plinth blocks, but adding the apron and the sill is heads above a picture frame treatment for windows. This is the best you can do with stock mouldings from a home center.

The first step in casing of this design begins with the window sill. You have to determine the length of the sill. To do so, take a short cutoff of the material you plan to use for the casing sides and mark the width on each side of the opening. Don't forget the reveal. Then measure the area between those two marks. Add 1¹/₂" to that length to arrive at the required length of the sill.

The sill has to be a certain width to make it work. What's the width? That depends. If you're working with the drywall wrapped scenario

3-9

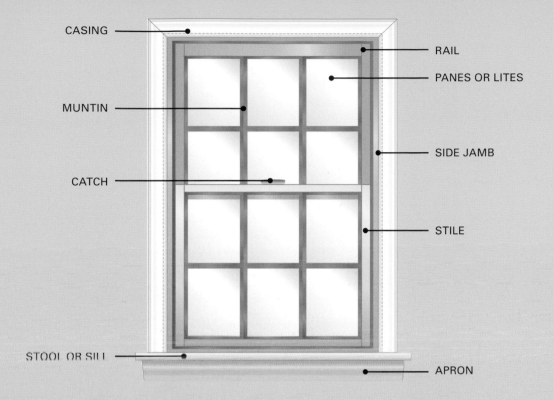

CASING

RAIL

PANES OR LITES

MUNTIN

SIDE JAMB

CATCH

STILE

STOOL OR SILL

APRON

described above, or if your uncased windows are flush with the wall surface, it has to be the thickness of the apron plus an appropriate overhang of about 3/4". With stock mouldings that will be sill material of 1⅜" at a minimum (Photo 3-9.)

If you're working with jamb extenders your sill width is the aforementioned 1⅜" plus any additional width needed to reach the window (fill in from the wall to the actual window). This is the case with many wood windows. While the windows had three sides flush with the wall, the sill had to reach back to the window.

Installing the sill can be tricky if the piece has to reach back to the window. In this case, you'll have to notch each end to fit tight to the window and to the wall. Place one end of the sill material tight to the window while also holding it to the edge of the opening. A mark at the wall surface will determine the amount that needs to be cut or notched at that end and the amount remaining for sill. Don't expect the opposite end to be the same

measurement. Walk through the steps to attain that notch area too. Next, position the sill equally spaced in the window opening. Mark the two locations, one on each end, where the wall starts back to the window. By connecting those two lines — the line determining the leftover sill and the location that the sill returns to the window — you arrive at the necessary notches. Make the cuts with a handsaw or with a jigsaw and you're ready to nail the sill in position. (See illustration above.)

To nail the sill in place you have to drill through the sill's width to drive nails into the studs behind the casing areas and drive at least one nail into the window frame. It's nearly impossible to use a nailing gun in this situation.

Next, cut the casing sides. These pieces are square cut where they meet, or sit on, the sill and have a 45° cut at their top ends. Set the appropriate reveal then nail the pieces to the wall and window (or jamb extenders).

3-10

3-11

An additional nail is required to properly install the case sides when using a sill or stool. Because the sill extends from the wall surface you can get under the ends of the side casings. From the underside of the sill, shoot a nail through the sill and into the casing. This ensures that the joint stays tight.

Finish the casing of the window by installing the head casing. Then fit and install an apron. An apron? It fits under the sill, flat to the wall and is generally cut on a small angle to add visual interest. (Photo 3-10.)

Use a wide apron with lots of details that is "returned" on itself. To return the moulding to the wall, cut the ends at a 45° cut to the wall, then cut a small piece that fits to the end while continuing the moulding profile back to the wall. (Photo 3-11.)

This can also be done to the sill as well, but I find that the best way to finish the sill is with a simple rounded edge. By using a rounded edge it's possible to round over the end grain of the piece without having to make any additional cuts or tedious fitting.

Need Extra Light in a Room

If you have a room in the house that's poorly lit or has no natural light, how about adding a window? (Photo 3-12.) No, I'm not suggesting that you cut holes in the exterior walls of the house, and I'm certainly not condoning skylights. (I think they are the most troublesome windows invented.) I'm suggesting that you add a window to one of your inside walls.

Frame an opening in an interior wall, install a window and allow sunlight to flood the room after it passes through the first room. In the photo on the facing page you see a small fixed glass window that does just that. The room is a small utility area, and the window adds elegance to the room needing light as well as the room that has light to share.

It's a simple process. Just be sure to install this window in a non-load-bearing wall. Locate the proposed window and draw the opening on your wall. (Using a small glass surface area is beneficial. You can then locate the window in an out-of-the-way spot.) There may be a bit of additional framing nec-

Jars of clay MERCHANDISE

① T-SHIRT
Natural with
maroon logo
100% cotton
One size fits all
$16.95

② BASEBALL CAP
Navy with
embroidered logo on
crown and Jars Of Clay
logo on back
Adjustable
$18.00

③ POSTER
18"x24" four color group image
$4.95
(not shown)

3-12

essary to get the hole ready. Remember to oversize the opening during the framing process.

Slide the window into the hole, add the trim as explained above and bingo — you've added light to an otherwise dark room and added another design element to both rooms. Stained glass is a great choice for this window.

From a building perspective I would only contemplate adding or replacing a window if the exterior of the house was wood. Having any type of brick or brick veneer is just going to complicate matters. (If I had brick and needed to change or add windows I would contact a company that specializes in that work.) In my opinion, this is work better left to professionals.

flip tip

Dressing up your windows will give your house an extra design element that will increase its look, feel and market value. Also, replace all cracked and broken window panes!

4

The front door of your home is the first element that a prospective buyer or potential renter will see as they walk up to your home. It has to be inviting and

door
trim and casings

make a lasting and blissful impression. Once inside, the interior doors become just as important. There's no way to enter or leave most rooms in your home without walking through some kind of door.

If that door is creaky, ill-fitting or unpleasant in design, visitors (and you) will be turned off. That may be the end of any possible sale or lease. And if it's your own home, what does that door say about you? Certainly it is a reflection on you and your family.

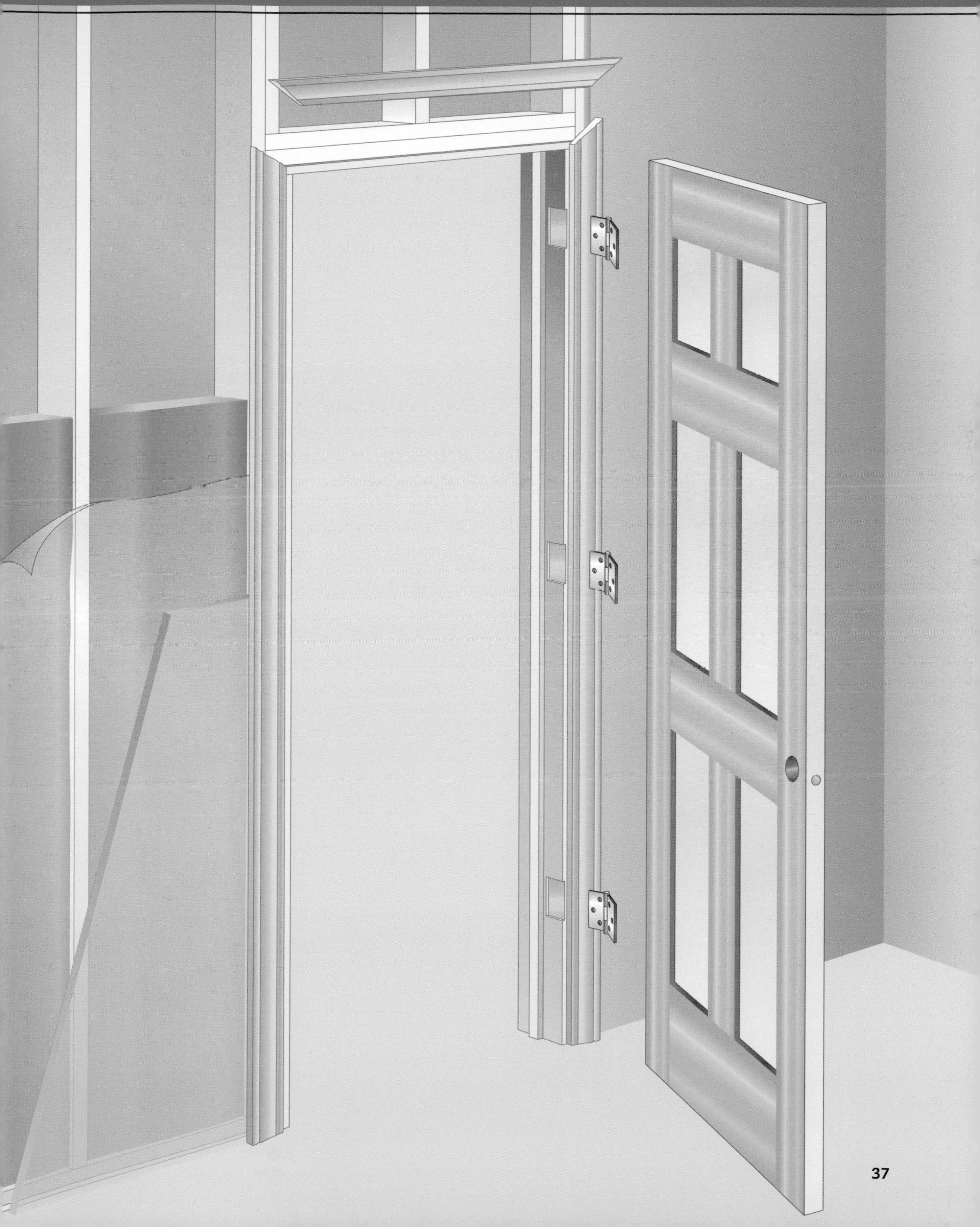

4-1

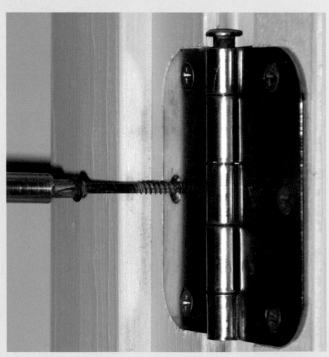

4-2

The doors in your home have to be stylish, well-designed and free-swinging. If they are not, it's time for a change. But, what do you do? Chances are, there are some doors that simply need adjustment. There are quick fixes that might work for some doors, but others will need to be replaced or updated.

Quick Fixes for your Doors

If your door is sagging — rubbing the floor as you try to open or closed it — and the problem isn't from a portion of the floor being raised, simply replacing a missing screw might be the answer. Take a quick look at the top hinge. Is there a screw missing, making the hinge hang loosly away from the jamb (the framework that the holds the door in the wall opening)? (Photo 4-1)

Replaceing the screw may pull the door tight to that top hinge-side corner and lift the door from touching the floor. It should make the reveal equal as you look around the door, and the doorknob should engage with the strike plate when shut. If this doesn't work, read on.

Try replacing the orginal $3/4"$ screw with a $2"$ screw into the center of the hinge. (Generally each hinge has three screws.) The jamb on the hinge side of the door should sit relatively close to the wall stud, so the new screw should be long enough to reach beyond the jamb, through any open space and into the stud framing to which the door is attached. You'll need to take a good bite into the stud because, essentially you're pulling the entire door frame back into its orginally installed position. (Photo 4-2)

4-3

4-4

What to do if the Quick Fixes Fail

So you've tried a couple quick fixes without any luck. Your only option now is to remove the door, try rehanging the old door or install a replacement (Think replacement. The cost to replace a door is not that high, but the chances of damaging the trim on the old door as it's removed are high.)

If you're renovating an old house and want to reuse the existing door, contact a professional

carpenter to complete the job. Locating the hinge positions, routing a matching hinge area on a new jamb, and drilling and installing a knob and lockset is not a job for the average homeowner.

But, you can do the deconstruction. First, remove the door slab from the door unit by removing the screws from the hinges on the door and frame. Then pull the trim from the unit. A hammer, pry bar and nail set will become your friends. However, before you grab those tools, get acquainted with a sharp utility knife. Start by scoring along the edges of the casings. (The casings are the part of the trim package that wraps around the door, are nailed to the frame or jambs, and are affixed to the walls.)

There are two places to cut with the knife. If you are working with a painted door and frame, there will be caulking along the inside edge of the casing as well as the outside edge where the trim meets the wall. (Photo 4-3.) If it's a stained door, you're more likely not to have any caulking to deal with, and, it will be easier to remove the casing. (See Photo 4-4.)

Carefully cut the caulking with the knife. In either case, painted or stained, cut the outside edge at the wall. If you attempt to pull the trim from the wall and the caulking or some of the finish still has a grip on the wall, it's possible to rip the drywall as the trim is pulled away. Take it slow and easy.

Position the pry bar on the wall to one side of the casing. Starting at the top, tap the bar until it slides under the casing or between the trim and the wall. Before applying any brute force, slide a thin wooden shim behind the bar. This will save the wall from damage as you pry.

Working slowly down the casing, gently pry the bar to loosen the trim. Move back to the top of the door and pry the trim off the jamb as you descend to the floor a second time. The nails used at the wall are likely 6d finish nails or 1½" – 2" nails from an air gun. The nails used to attach the trim to the jamb will be 2d finish nails or 1" nails from an air

DOOR TERMINOLOGY

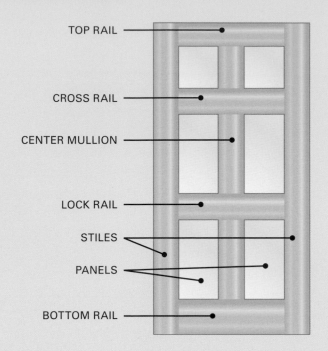

TOP RAIL

CROSS RAIL

CENTER MULLION

LOCK RAIL

STILES

PANELS

BOTTOM RAIL

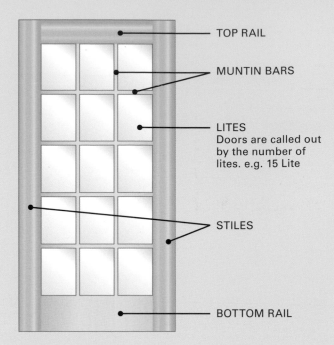

TOP RAIL

MUNTIN BARS

LITES
Doors are called out
by the number of
lites. e.g. 15 Lite

STILES

BOTTOM RAIL

gun. If the door was factory-cased (a split-jamb style door), the trim might be attached to the jamb with small staples.

Repeat this process on the other side. Once the trim is removed it's time to separate the door frame from the opening. You can use a nail set to punch the nails through the frame and free the jambs, or turn to electric power and use a reciprocating saw to cut the nails between the casing and the wall studs. Then, pull the frame from the opening.

If You're Thinking Replacement, How do You Know What to Get?

Doors are sized and talked about in feet and inches. This confuses some people. I once worked with a purchaser who was looking all over the city for a special door. He was looking for a 30" × 30" door. When he told me none was to be found in that size,

I told him that the door needed was a 3'-0" × 3'-0" door. He didn't last long with the company.

When I was building homes, ordinary interior doors were installed in a 2/0, 2/4, 2/6, 2/8 or 3/0 size. (Other sizes are available but become special order items.) The first number is the feet and the second is the inches. The door in the above scenario would have called out as a 3/0 × 3/0 door. You can see how he decided to look for a 30" square door. This is not to say that you won't happen upon doors in other sizes, but it's not that common.

Here's the rub. If you measure the existing opening, you're not going to get the correct size door. Why? Because doors are roughed-in (the opening is constructed) about 2" – 2½" larger than the actual door slab measurement. The additional opening is for the frame and the area required to correctly install the unit. If you measure an opening that is 32" and buy a door that is 2/8 you're going to make a second trip to the lumberyard or home center. To get the correct door size move down 2" in width. A 32" opening requires a 2/6 door.

INTERIOR DOOR OPTIONS

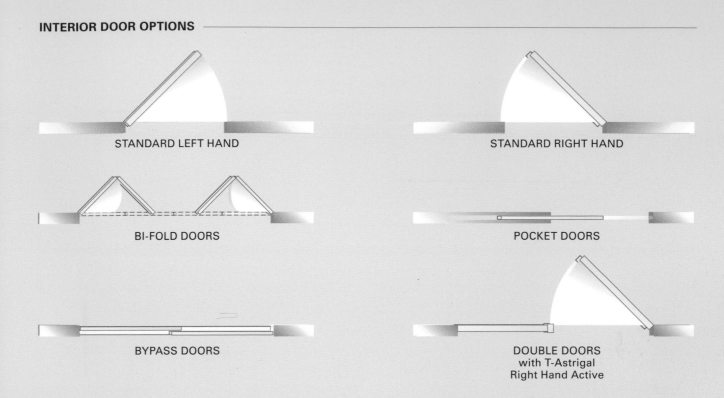

STANDARD LEFT HAND

STANDARD RIGHT HAND

BI-FOLD DOORS

POCKET DOORS

BYPASS DOORS

DOUBLE DOORS
with T-Astrigal
Right Hand Active

The height of doors has changed over the past decade. The standard height for a door used to be 6/8 (that's feet and inches again), and the opening in the wall was framed with 2" of extra height. Now doors are available in multiple heights. Remember to check that measurement as well.

Adjusting the Rough Opening

Is your rough door opening sized to work with a standard door unit? Maybe not if the original door was hung years back when the units were custom-made on the jobsite. It's important to have the correct rough opening. It makes the door installation much easier. You may have to close down the opening or widen the area to allow for a proper fit.

Closing down the opening is simple. Depending on the amount you need to close, you can use a thin piece of plywood ripped to the stud width or any varying thickness of material needed to complete the task. I've added anywhere from a 1/4"

piece of plywood up to another stud which is 1½"-thick. Just remember that any larger amount you close will need to have the drywall added and the wall surface finished like the rest of the wall. Thin additions are sometimes covered by the door trim.

Increasing the size of the door opening is not quite as easy. You may catch a break if the wall is not, I repeat not, a load-bearing wall. If this is the case you can remove one of the cripple, which is a stud that fits under the header and next to the support stud. If you don't need to remove the entire thickness of the stud, simply remove the stud and add a filler to arrive at the appropriate opening. Remember to plumb the hinge side of the opening.

If the door is to swing correctly, the hinge side of the door must be plumb. What's plumb? Using a level that is at least 4' long, make sure the stud against which the hinge side of the door attaches is straight up and down. If the stud leans toward or away from the opening, your door will not swing properly. That's not good. To plumb the stud you

TYPICAL PANEL DOORS (flat or raised panels)

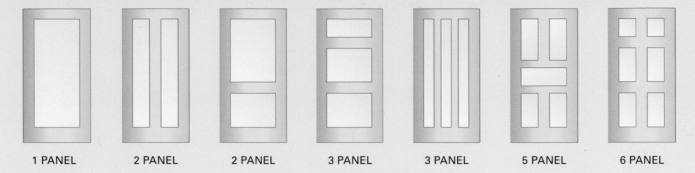

| 1 PANEL | 2 PANEL | 2 PANEL | 3 PANEL | 3 PANEL | 5 PANEL | 6 PANEL |

may need to add a few shims. Bring it to plumb before installing the door.

If your wall is load-bearing, change the prospective door down one size (move from a 2/8 to a 2/6 door), and don't mess with the wall framing.

What about the swing of the door? This is actually called *handing* a door. Is it a right-hand swing or a left-hand swing? I fuddled with this for a while before finding a solution that worked for me. Here's my process.

Stand with your back against the hinge side of the door. If you mimic the swing of the door by moving your left arm, that's called a left-hand door. If you move your right arm as the door moves — it's a right hand door. Seems easy doesn't it? I mixed this up more than once before understanding the correct method to hand a door.

Door Styles and Designs

Having six-panel doors in your home was once the rage in my area. A few years ago the trend was using flush birch doors. Times change. Designs change. If you are replacing a door you must select a door that matches the existing look or that is at least similar to the door being removed. (See the illustration below.)

A trip to the home center will uncover various designs and also prices. Why the different prices

for doors that appear to be the same? Check out the weight. Chances are that one of the doors is a solid-core door while the less expensive one is a hollow-core door. A solid-core door has a solid wood core with veneer applied to both faces. A hollow-core door has a honeycomb-looking core made of corrugated cardboard with veneer applied to both faces. Unless you are working in an upscale home, I'd bet that most interior doors leading into the bedrooms, bathrooms and other areas of the house are hollow-core. Make a note of this before

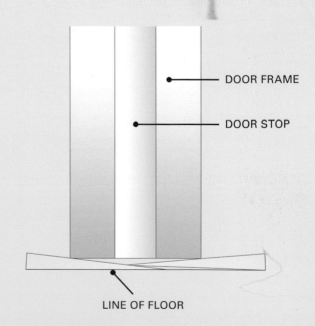

DOOR FRAME

DOOR STOP

LINE OF FLOOR

Insert shims from both sides of the door casing. This ensures equal pressure.

tion that is simply the trim mounted to a part of the jamb and a second section that comprises the balance of the jamb with the trim and door slab in place. The hanging operation for both of these doors is both similar and different.

Hanging the Pre-hung Door

The opening for the unit is ready to go. That means the hinge side of the opening is plumb and the opening is sized correctly.

Remove the packaging from the door unit. Free the door so it can open and close. Position the frame into the opening and slide the hinge side tight to the stud. Center the jamb (both edges should be flush with the finished wall surface), then drive one nail on the hinge side at the top of the jamb. The nail should be through the door stop so as not to interfere with the operation of the door. Next add another nail at the bottom of the jamb at the lower hinge. Don't set these nails flush just yet.

Carefully close the door and check the reveal around the door slab. It should be even, about the thickness of a nickel, or at worst the non-hinge side should need to be raised to gain that reveal at the top edge of the door. If that's the case you're ready to move on. If you find an uneven gap or reveal at the top edge of the door, you need to raise the hinge side slightly. So, pull the nails loose (but not out) and slide a shim, one from each side of the wall, under the jamb between the jamb and the floor. Slide the two shims toward each other slightly raising the hinge-side jamb. (See drawing facing page.) Tap the nails in and check the reveal again. Repeat if necessary.

If all looks correct, nail the hinge side to the stud with one nail on either side of the door stop, through the jamb and into the stud. (See large photo on previous page.)

Next, secure the non-hinge jamb to its stud. To do this you again need wooden shims. Position the

you venture out shopping. Knowing if it's solid or hollow might save you a second trip to the store.

When you do go shopping, another thought to keep in mind is, what type of jambs are on the rest of the doors in the house. What type of jamb? They're wooden right? Right, but doorjambs come in two styles. One is a pre-hung door (meaning the door slab is attached to the frame at the hinges) where the door is hung on the frame or jamb and is ready for you to install and add casing. The second type is called a split-jamb door. This design is also pre-hung, but the casing is already in place. With this type of door you need to select the trim around the door when you purchase the unit.

A split-jamb door is just what it says. The jamb is split into two pieces. Once uncrated from the packaging you can separate the jamb into one sec-

jamb so it's flush with the wall surfaces, then drive a few nails through the jamb. Nail through the door stop and space the nails evenly from the top edge of the jamb to the floor.

Start at the top of the door. Close it to evaluate the reveal. Slide two shims in from opposing sides, between the stud and the jamb, until they snug up to the jamb. Locate the shims just above the nails, placing one set of shims behind the door's strike plate area.

Adjust the shims (sliding the two inward causes the jamb to move closer to the door slab while sliding the two out loosens the fit) as you watch the reveal around the door. When the gap appears consistent add a nail through the jamb, the shims, and into the stud to hold everything in place. Then, nail through the jamb on both sides of the door stop holding the frame in place. (See inset photo previous page.)

Sometimes it's necessary to add the shims to the center of the top of the jamb to ensure a solid fit of the door casing. If necessary, push the shims in place as you've done with the shims in the jamb.

Add the casing to the frame. Start by fitting and attaching the casing to each side of the door frame, cutting a 45° angle at the top end of the pieces. Next, fit the head casing to the frame matching the 45° cuts.

Hanging a Split-Jamb Door

After reading how to hang a pre-hung door, I think you'll be more interested in using split-jamb doors in your home. It's worth the effort to find these doors even though home centers seem to shy away from carrying this design. You may have to find them at a local lumber yard.

Installing a split-jamb door is easier than installing a pre-hung door. Once you get the door home, unwrap it from the packaging and pull the nails that hold it closed. Also, remove the staples that hold the jamb together.

In split-jamb doors the jamb separates into two pieces. One half is simply a partial frame with the casing applied while the other half is the balance

Install shims at critical pressure points, such as behind the hinges and the strike plate. Note the shims installed from opposite directions.

I like the older style treatment for casing and baseboard work in homes. A simple way to update the look is to add fluted casings around your doors. (The same treatment is used for windows – see chapter four.)

of the frame with the door hung and the casing already applied.

Begin with the half holding the door. Place the door into the opening and slide the unit tight to the hinge side. Check the fit of the door to the frame. You're looking at the reveal again. The area to check this time is the hinge side and the top. Don't worry about the lock side yet.

If the top reveal is good, add a couple of nails through the casing at the top corner of the hinge side and near the lower hinge. The door will hold in place with just this amount of work.

If the top reveal is correct (look for that nickel-thick spacing) or tight, you are still OK to nail. The only problem is if the reveal is too large at the top. If this is the case you need to pull the nails. Rock

the top of the door toward the hinge side, or slide the bottom hinge corner away from the stud (either one will adjust the door the necessary direction) until the reveal is equal. Drive the nails at the top of the hinge side or at the lower hinge.

Once the reveal is good, add nails to the casing on the hinge side of the unit and along the top. Starting at the top of the knob edge of the door, work the reveal to an even gap as you add nails through the casing and into the studs. One-half of the door unit is installed.

Working from the side of the door that isn't attached to the wall, add shims to build out the studs to the jamb on all sides of the door opening. Once you achieve a snug fit, drive nails through the door stop to secure the unit to the opening. Space the nails evenly along the length of the jamb, locating a shim behind each hinge as well as behind the lock area on the non-hinge side. (See photo facing page.)

Cut off any shims that protrude past the wall surface, then slide the second half of the jamb into position and lock the two pieces together. Nail through the pre-attached casing and the split portion of the jamb, and the job is finished.

USING SPECIAL CASING TRIM

With the split-jamb design you have somewhat limited casing choices, but if you're installing the pre-hung units there are many design options. There are a myriad of choices for casing the doors. Your imagination is your only limit.

Fluted casing can be purchased where you buy lumber and materials, or it can be made from raw stock and a router. (See chapter five for information on fluting.) Using this special feature along with plinth blocks at the base of the casing — and the top if you choose — is certainly an eye-catching design. I use the plinths at the bottom then add a solid top piece that is slightly thicker than the fluted pieces.

Add a cap moulding above the head casing that extends beyond each side of the frame as a finishing touch. That piece is returned to the wall — the moulding edge rounds the corners and is tight to the wall. Add a simple strip of straight moulding up each side of the door and the look is complete.

I'm sure that you have many thoughts, ideas and designs that will look great around your doors. There's no need to stick with standard mouldings. Look at various magazines for additional design ideas.

PLINTH
BLOCK

flip tip

To accurately fit the head casing, cut one end at the 45° angle, then flip the head casing so that the pointed end of the cut is down. Align this point to the point of the side casing, then correctly mark the point on the opposite end of the head casing. This gives you an accurate length, but you may need to fine-tune the final fit.

5

Throughout your home there is one common theme that ties the individual rooms together in one coherent collection. That theme is the room trim or mouldings.

room
trim

Those profiles include, but aren't limited to, crown mouldings, chair rails, baseboards and casings. These mouldings, when added to your home, have the potential for immediate reward. They upgrade the look of your rooms and suggest that special care has gone into your property.

What are these mouldings? In the past, the mouldings used in houses were wood pieces that were shaped and cut to achieve a specific look. Woodworkers used hand planes to produce various profiles on the jobsite while wide pieces of trim were made in shops, where apprentices pulled large planes, under the guidance of master artisans. Many mouldings were specific to houses or homebuilders. Carpenters discovered how to combine

machine-made mouldings to create complex profiles in an infinite variety of designs.

Mouldings, when viewed separately, are not that impressive. However, view them in a room that is completely finished and the effect can be astounding. Plus, they distinguish your property from others. Simple profiles that are no more than 2"– 4" wide suddenly transform into continuous lines of trim that separate the walls from the floors or the ceilings from the walls.

How are mouldings used in housing? Primarily they're used to transition from one plane to another. Baseboards to conceal the gap between your floor and wall, while casings hide the opening between and around door frames where they meet the wall.

In addition, mouldings like chair rails, for example, are positioned to divide different materials such as paint and wallpaper. Chair rails accent a room while protecting walls from scuffs and dents. By manipulating these mouldings you can influence how people perceive your room.

Is Wood The Only Choice?

The simple, resounding answer is no. Although mouldings began as profiled wood created by skilled craftsman, today many materials are shaped by machines.

With that being said, it is best to use wood mouldings when staining the trim in your home. Wood mouldings are tried and true in the home-building industry and have been around for a long time.

Finger-jointed mouldings need to be painted, as the joint looks unsightly if stain is used.

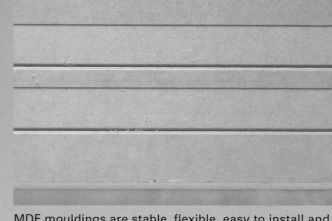

MDF mouldings are stable, flexible, easy to install and take paint well. However, they are heavy and difficult to cut using hand tools.

Wood can be made into a larger variety of shapes with the router bits available in wood working and it holds its shape well. If a chair rail is bumped, it won't easily get dented. Most homeowners have the resources to cut, fit and nail trim into place. Solid wood mouldings are the grand daddy of all mouldings. Everything else is new by comparison.

Finger joints can be used to join small pieces of wood into long stock that's then moulded into different profiles. Finger-jointed moulding should be used as painted trim. If they are stained, the joints stand out and detract from the look of the trim.

Today, medium-density fiberboard (MDF) is used to make nearly all moulding profiles. Are the products worth using as trim in your home? Yes and no. On the plus side, MDF trim is always primed or painted before you buy it. This saves you a step in the finishing process. It costs less than wood or finger-jointed mouldings. MDF mouldings don't split if nailed near an edge, and the material has some flexibility, which is nice if you're adding trim to a bowed wall.

On the minus side, MDF has a tendency to bulge slightly as a nail penetrates its surface. You can flatten the bulge by lightly sanding or scraping with your putty knife. Also, MDF trim is heavier than its counterparts, which makes coping cuts more difficult.

A plaster moulding (left) and a plastic moulding (right). It's my opinion that mouldings made of these materials should be used above eye level to avoid being easily damaged.

The Use of Plastic

Home centers carry some mouldings that are plastic, and upon first look, you can't tell the difference between them and their wooden cousins. You can get away with using plastic mouldings, only where paint is the final topcoat.

The profiles are extruded and in some cases a white painted finish is applied. Plastic mouldings are also available in a textured finish that resembles oak or some other hardwood. What's the advantage of using alternative materials for your home's trim mouldings? It costs less than solid wood pieces, is a renewable resource and requires minimal maintainance. Plastic profiles are only limited by the manufacturer's imagination. There are no knives to grind as there would be for a moulding machine that makes wood profiles.

Another plastic option is Fypon. This is a high-density expanded polystyrene product that is lightweight and can be shaped to any profile. I've used this moulding to create a beautiful room décor, and I installed every piece with glue. With no nail holes there were no nail holes to fill. Once installed, the trim was complete. If you want something other than white trim, simply paint it a color as your last step.

Plaster was shaped into a design and used as mouldings in a room where painted wood mouldings were dominant. In fact, some early mouldings were made from plaster with a small amount of horsehair added for strength.

Understanding the Different Players

Certain mouldings are used in certain areas. Let's take a look at a few of the important types to explore their profiles and shapes.

We'll look at cove, chair rail, casings and baseboards. Keep in mind that even though these mouldings are normally used in certain posi-

tions, they can be stacked, flipped and/or rotated and used outside their normal neighborhood. Baseboard, normally used at the floor, can be used in a complex crown moulding. Chair rail, along with trims such as shelf-edge moulding or screen moulding, is used to create a look that is similar to wainscot. Mouldings can also be used with square edge boards to add a design feature to a room. Let your imagination run wild.

STANDARD CROWN

BUILT-UP CROWN MOULDING

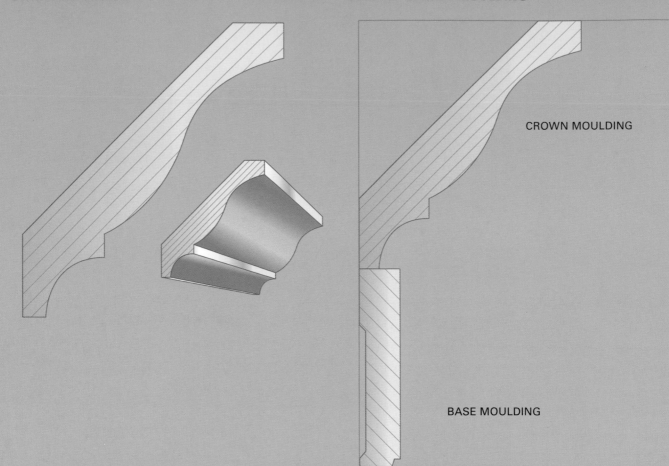

CROWN MOULDING

BASE MOULDING

Crown Moulding

When you walk the trim and moulding aisles at the home center, one of the most prevalent profiles is going to be crown moulding. It's primary use is to divide the ceiling from the walls, and it's available in many sizes and profiles ranging from 1⅝" to 7⅜" (crown moulding is measured in width). Each of these sizes can be made with various profiles.

Interestingly, this is the only well-known moulding with a single-task description. I cannot remember when I've ever used a piece of crown moulding anywhere but at the intersection of the ceiling and wall.

If you look at the profile, it becomes clear why this is true. Crown moulding does not have edges that are square to the flat back of the stock. If it were nailed with its back against the wall, its edges would be raised from the wall, leaving an awkward finish to the trim.

However, crown moulding can be used with other mouldings to create some fantastic designs.

ings. Invert the baseboard, placing the routed edge downward, and install it as the first step in the design. Add a piece of crown moulding to increase the size of the trim, and it's more apt to catch your eye. This is only the beginning of what could be created.

One reason that crown moulding works so well is that as you enter a room your eye is caught by the moulding at the intersection of the wall and ceiling. Therefore, if a design briefly catches your eye, it accomplishes the purpose. The baseboard/crown moulding combination would net a bit over 3" of moulding in standard design.

Another design idea is fooling the eye. Mouldings spaced apart is a great idea to inexpensively spruce up a room. Choose a small profile moulding that casts a shadow, place it on the wall about 6" – 10" below the ceiling. The exact location depends on the room height. (If the rooms are 8'0" or less, position the moulding closer to the 6" range.)

Next, paint the moulding and the area above it the same color as the ceiling. This appears to be a wide crown moulding or at minimum, a multiple stack setup. It's guaranteed to catch the eye and present an elegant interior without using crown. Of course, adding the crown into the wall/ceiling corner improves the look that much more.

Let your mind work freely and I'll bet you can come up with a profile, be it stacked or spaced, that improves your room's appearance. It's a fast and effective way to add value to a home.

Creating Cove Designs

While crown moulding doesn't get used often in combination with different profiles to concoct a multiple stacked design, there are many other players that are used as types of crown moulding. Some are used along with the crown in a multiple-step or build-up moulding, and others work by themselves with a crown moulding near by.

Baseboard is the most commonly used moulding to help produce the multiple-step crown mould-

Lowering the height of a chair rail makes a small room appear larger because your eye perceives the ceiling as being higher than it is.

SIMPLE CHAIR RAIL

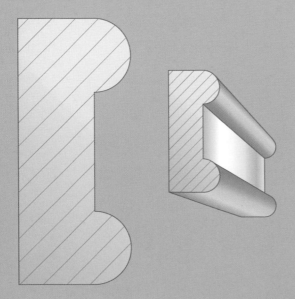

Chair Rail

A simple definition of chair rail is a horizontal moulding, used simply as decoration, and placed part way up a wall to protect the wall's surface from chair backs. While that's true, it's also much more than that.

At first chair rail was used to protect the walls, but somewhere along its path, it became a major player in fancy trim carpentry and decoration. Today chair rail is used at various heights to produce more impact in design, it is the top edge of many faux wainscot designs, and it is the focal dividing line for paint and wallpaper.

Installing a frame between the chair rail and base moulding, then painting that area a different color than the upper wall is an inexpensive way to dress up a room.

Use a chair rail as a divider between two different wall treatments.

The standard height for chair rail is around 36" based on the back height of dining room chairs. That's a guideline, not a rule. I've installed this moulding at 24" off the finished floor where the impact on the design scheme was incredible. The room's overall size appears to grow in size. The lower rail drew the eye downward, making the ceiling of the room seem higher. This is a great way to increase the expanse of a small room.

Chair rail can also be used to create the look of wainscot without applying solid wood to the walls. The process is quick and much less expensive than solid wood paneling. Simply install the chair rail along the walls in an entry hall or dining room. Create squares in a picture frame effect with small trim pieces such as shelf edging, positioning them between the lower edge of the chair rail and the top edge of any baseboard. The look is elegant, and the cost is negligible.

Most dining rooms are the elegant room of the house — the area for entertaining and serving meals to guests. That room needs to stand out. If you have remodeling to do, updating or sprucing up the dining room is a great place to invest your money. New paint and wallpaper is the answer.

Paint alone helps but doesn't complete the job. Wallpaper adds a certain design, but can become over-powering quickly. The answer is a combination of the two. I'm not talking of painting some walls and adding wallpaper to the others, although I've seen accent walls (a single wall in a room that is different from the others) work great. Instead, install a chair rail, then paint above it while adding wallpaper below. The chair rail is the dividing line between the paint and the wallpaper.

BASIC CHAIR RAIL

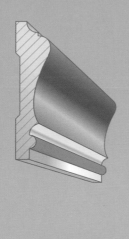

STANDARD CASING

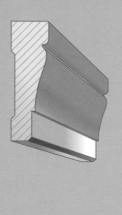

BUILT-UP CHAIR RAIL

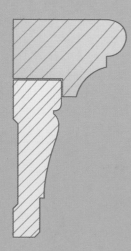

CAP MOLDING

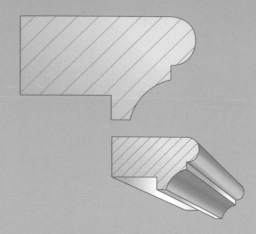

Chair-Rail Variations

Chair rail can be as simple as a piece of screen moulding (although I wouldn't suggest this if you are flipping a house or if you want someone to actually buy the property) or as complex as a stack of profiles.

Basic chair rail (see the illustration), has a nice profile and is approximately $2^{1}/_{2}$"-wide. This profile has been around for at least the past 40 years. I've used it many times. You can't go wrong with stock such as this.

As I mentioned before, you can use a profile that's not as fancy. The simple chair rail is only $1^{3}/_{4}$"-wide and the profile appears as a flat piece of stock with two half-rounds at either edge. Certainly, this is better than flat stock alone, but remember that your aim is to find a buyer for your home or at least to create a more inviting area for entertaining.

I like to install a chair rail that is a notch or two above the standard. This design requires two stacked pieces for the rail. Believe it or not, this design starts with a piece of door or window casing.

The casing, when held flat to the wall and run horizontal, with the wider edge facing up, is the perfect base for this design. Top off the casing with a cap moulding for a great design.

If you add the width of standard casing to that of the cap moulding, you get a stacked profile that measures about 3". But, because casing profiles are available in many sizes, you can design a profile to fit your idea. This is precisely why I believe that can you set your home apart from all others when using mouldings.

Casings

Casings act primarily as door or window trim. They bridge the gaps left after the installation of windows and doors. But they are so much more.

Due to the many different sizes and designs of casing, you have abundant opportunity to put your mark on your trim carpentry. I found casing styles and sizes at one supplier that ranged in width from $2^{1}/4$" to over $5^{1}/2$". There were also over 50 different designs produced.

Those were custom profiles. Strolling down the aisle of my local home center I discovered 26 different designs of stock mouldings. The sizes ranged from $2^{1}/4$" to $3^{1}/4$". Clearly you can select casing profiles that display your individual decorating concepts.

And if those choices aren't quite what you have in mind, you can always make your own design. One of my favorite ideas for making elegant casings is to use fluted stock. If you look for this design at a home center, I doubt you'll find many like it, if you find it at all. Learn how to make fluted trim and you'll always be able to add a special touch to your home. It just might be what closes the deal.

Fluting with a Router

Taking your casing to the next level is as easy as running a router. I'll explain the process using a hand-held router. Any router will work when creating flutes, but there are a few accessories that

you need to make it easy, including the proper router bit.

The router bit needed for this job is what's known as a core box bit or a round nose bit. The size of the bit is a matter of choice, but I find a $3/4"$ bit most useful. With a $3/4"$ bit you don't have to cut the entire $3/4"$. In fact, you will seldom use the full width. Depending on the depth of the cut, you can create grooves that are anywhere from $3/8"$ wide to those that take advantage of the $3/4"$ bit size. Of course, having a couple of sizes makes almost any width groove attainable.

Next, you need a guide fence that fits your router. If your router doesn't come with a guide fence, pick one up that works with your specific router. The fence runs along the edge of your board and allows you to set the distance from the edge to the center of the bit. First figure the distance and set the fence, then you're ready to create fluted trim.

The easiest setup for routing fluted stock is to use an odd number of flutes. Three flutes is the basic design. Set up and route a flute at the dead-center of the stock. Next, move the router bit toward the edge of the stock or away from the center. Try to establish the groove near the center of the remaining flat area. Cut the groove with the fence against one side, then turn the board and make a second cut with the router bit positioned on the opposite side. This results in a three-flute board with equal spacing between the side and center flutes.

You could cut five flutes in your profile. Again, start with the center groove. Proceed as if routing three grooves, but this time establish the grooves about $1/4"$ away from that center groove (run both edges), then create one more groove per side that is also spaced $1/4"$ away from the previous groove.

It's much easier to establish the flutes around the center groove than it is to establish equal spacing with an even number of flutes because finding the center is simple math.

STANDARD BASEBOARD ———————— **BUILT-UP BASEBOARD** ————————

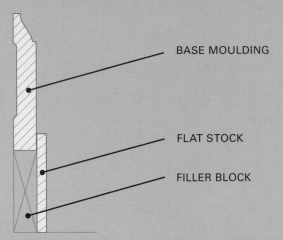

BASE MOULDING

FLAT STOCK

FILLER BLOCK

Baseboard

In every home there is an area where the walls meet the floors — it has to happen. The floors are wood, carpet or some other man-made covering — they are never drywall. It's because of that change in material and the geometric plane that we need baseboards.

Floor coverings expand and contract as humidity rises and falls. This seasonal movement is another reason baseboard exists. Knowing that the floor will expand, you leave an expansion gap between the floor and the wall. These baseboards, which run horizontally, cover any gap between the two expanses.

Baseboards also protect the wall from vacuum cleaners, everyday cleaning tools and sliding chairs. When people used to clean their floors with water and a mop, the term mop-board was often used. The mopboard kept the mop and water from surging into the wall area and causing damage. Today, I still hear folks use mopboard in place of baseboard.

How do you choose the right baseboard? As you roam the home center you'll find many different designs and styles. Choose baseboards that are thinner than the casings. This is generally

not a hard thing to do because most baseboards are designed to end or begin at the door casings. Also match the profile design to balance your trim mouldings. You don't want a ranch style baseboard used with a colonial casing. Baseboards should tie the room together.

Finally, use the baseboard as another way to express your creativity. Select a wide baseboard to draw more attention to the trim. Just remember that as the moulding grows wider, the price grows larger. I've seen baseboard designs that involve stacked pieces. This also adds to the cost of your job, so plan accordingly.

The best example of this type of design is to place a row of standard baseboard around the room about 5" above the finished floor to the top edge of the moulding. Then add another piece of flat stock ($1/4$" – $3/8$" in thickness) so that the second piece covers from the floor up to $1/2$" onto the baseboard. In order for the flat stock to fit correctly, it's necessary to build out the area below the baseboard with spacers that equal the thickness of the base moulding. This is done with scrap. The extra shadow line created has a powerful effect when you see the profile painted in a finished room. (See illustration above.)

Installation is Key

We've looked at various moulding types, profiles and designs. Without a basic understanding of the installation process this knowledge is useless. You might be thinking, "How hard can it be?" And, you would be mostly right.

I'm not going to spend much time on nailing the mouldings. That explains itself. However, fitting the trim in place and making the necessary cuts to install it correctly is another matter.

The major horizontally-positioned mouldings (crown, chair rail and baseboard), are all installed in the same manner — three easy steps to a finished job. Begin by laying out the location. We'll use chair rail as a demonstration. At one corner, mark the height of the bottom edge of the moulding. Move to a second corner and also mark that height. Likewise, work the entire room, making a mark at each stopping or starting point of the moulding.

With a friend, use a chalk line to snap a straight line between each of the mating points. Pull the line from the door casing and hold it tightly. (While away from the wall, flick the line a time or two to remove the majority of the chalk.) Then move into position, hold the line at the marks and make a light snap to transfer the line to the wall. First removing the accumulated chalk on the line keeps the walls clean and avoids a general mess.

Next find the studs in the wall. If you do not nail into the studs, the trim will bend from the wall at best, and fall to the floor at worst. Neither scenario is good. Tap on the wall to help find the studs, then use the nail to assure the location. Work just above the layout line. Any holes are covered by the installed moulding. Once found, make a pencil mark just below the layout line — a mark that you can see while holding the moulding in place.

Start with the longest run of moulding in the room. Cut this first piece with both ends square

Use a coping saw to cut a coped joint. This cut takes some practice because the saw needs to be angled back from the front edge of the moulding. Also, the saw needs to be guided along the profile.

This is a completed coping cut. The moulding at left is shown from the backside of the piece. Note how much the cut needs to be angled. This ensures that the coped edge fits snugly against the mating moulding.

so it fits between the walls. A slightly long piece ensures that the moulding stays to the wall once positioned. Use your air-powered gun to drive 6d finish nails through the moulding and into the studs. Two nails per stud, spaced near the top and bottom, is perfect.

Fitting the corners

It's all been straightforward so far, although you might be wondering why the corners aren't cut at a 45° angle to fit with the next piece, which is also cut at a 45° angle to complete a 90° turn at the corner. If they're installed properly, inside corners need to be coped because most corners are not exactly 90°. And, as mentioned before, wood expands and contracts. Using a coped joint allows for slight movement of the wood.

What is a coped joint? Take a look at the photo at right. This is a completed cope fit. It looks like a perfect 90° corner, but notice the square edge at the top of the left-hand piece. It extends into the proposed corner, and the right-hand piece is cut to fit around that first piece.

Coped joints are cut with a coping saw. The joint on the end of the mating piece is backcut at

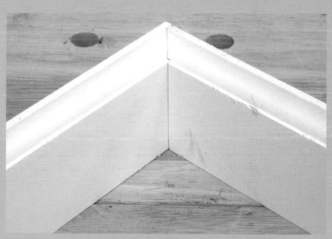

The piece on the right has been coped to fit the piece on the left. After some practice, you'll want to use this method for installing all of your mouldings.

45° so that the front edge makes a clean line when installed against the other moulding.

Easy enough, right? Just remember, if the moulding has a more complex profile, the coping cut is going to be more intricate.

Install each piece of trim in the same way. When you fit into an inside corner make a coping cut at one end and square cut at the other end as you work around the room. Of course, any piece that fits to a door or window casing is going to be cut square on that end.

If necessary, use blocks to fill the gap between the bottom of the drywall and the floor when installing baseboard.

INSTALLING BASEBOARD ————————————

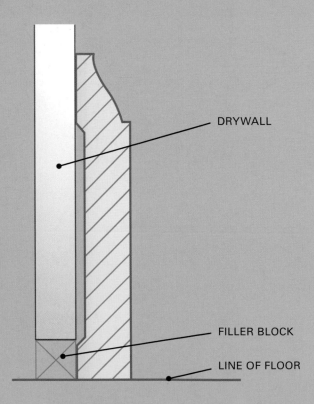

DRYWALL

FILLER BLOCK

LINE OF FLOOR

Baseboard installation

Each moulding has a few details that require additional work when installing. For example, if you install a two-piece chair rail, the lower portion of the moulding is installed as explained on the previous page. But, the cap moulding is installed with the inside corners cut at 45° and fit as tight as possible.

If you're installing baseboard into a recently constructed home, you may find a small gap where the wallboard or drywall meets the floor. Some of today's homes have walls constructed that are $1/2"$ taller than 8'0".

The back of standard baseboard moulding is profiled leaving a slightly raised portion at the base. That portion is about $1/2"$ in width. As a result, the baseboard twists back at the base as it's installed because the raised back portion slides below the drywall edge. To remedy this install $1/2"$ square × 2"-long blocks at the stud locations. The blocks fill in gaps so the baseboard won't twist.

Crown moulding

When cutting mouldings with a miter saw, crown moulding can be tricky because of its complex profile. All the other mouldings simply lie flat at the miter saw when they are cut, whether it's on a 45° angle or just square.

Some carpenters recommend that crown be laid flat as it's cut, if you have a compound miter saw. To accomplish this you need to tip the saw to a specific bevel angle and then rotate the degrees of the miter cut to another specific angle. It's rather tricky, and each moulding has its own set of angles.

I recommend cutting crown moulding as shown in the photo at right. Place the moulding at the miter saw in an orientation that is upside down and backward to the way it's installed. (Crown moulding is installed with the cove next to the wall.) Use this miter saw cut only for outside corners. Cope inside corners as explained on page 63.

Crown moulding can be cut using a miter saw without compound cutting capability. The moulding is positioned upside down and backward. Set the miter cut at 45°, hold the moulding against the saw's fence and table, and make the cut.

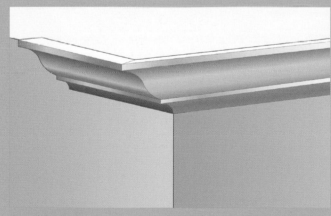

Outside corner crown moulding can be cut using a power miter saw.

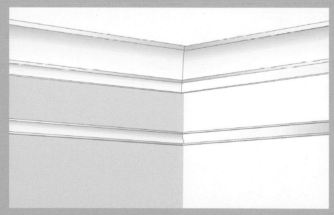

Inside corner crown moulding needs to be coped using a coping saw.

Create dramatic built-up crown moulding with Freud's wide-crown moulding bits

In 2006, Freud introduced a selection of six Wide Crown Moulding Bits that allowed professional woodworkers and woodworking enthusiasts to create traditional $5\frac{1}{2}$" crown moulding to add beauty and value to a home, using only the tools found in a common woodworking shop. Never before had it been possible to create wide crown moulding like this on the jobsite in any wood species that was desired. Now, Freud has taken it one step further.

Trim carpenters, remodelers and any woodworking enthusiast can now mill crown moulding of almost any size, adding beautiful detail to rooms with the highest ceilings. What's required? Just a $2\frac{1}{4}$" HP or larger router, a sturdy router table and fence and a selection of bits from Freud's Architectural Millwork System.

"We received great feedback from the industry on our wide crown moulding bits," asserts Cliff Paddock, Director of New Product Development – Cutting Tools. "However, newer homes are being constructed with 9' — or taller — ceilings and for crown moulding to truly make the desired dramatic effect, the crown had to be wider than $5\frac{1}{2}$"." By utilizing a variety of Freud's architectural millwork bits, the sky is literally the limit on how wide the crown can be built."

The key to beautiful built-up crown moulding is Freud's unique Wide Crown Moulding Bits. The six wide crown bits mill a choice of nine different profiles of genuine $5\frac{1}{2}$" wide crown moulding. Then choose from the wide range of bits in Freud's Millwork System — or even use other decorative bits from Freud's huge bit selection — to add horizontal elements between the crown and ceiling and vertical elements between the crown and wall. The result is a dramatic moulding with a width of 7", 8", 9" or more!

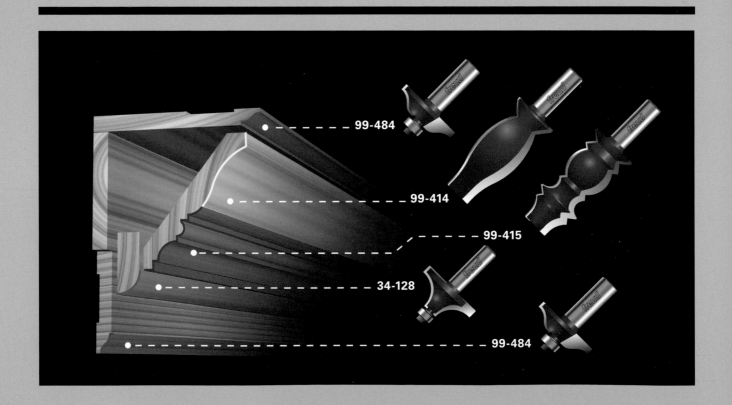

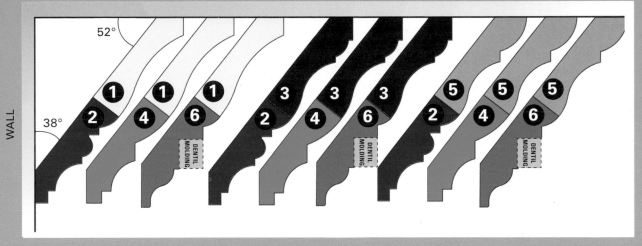

CEILING

52°

WALL

38°

A total of 9 different combinations can be created with
the Wide Crown Molding System.

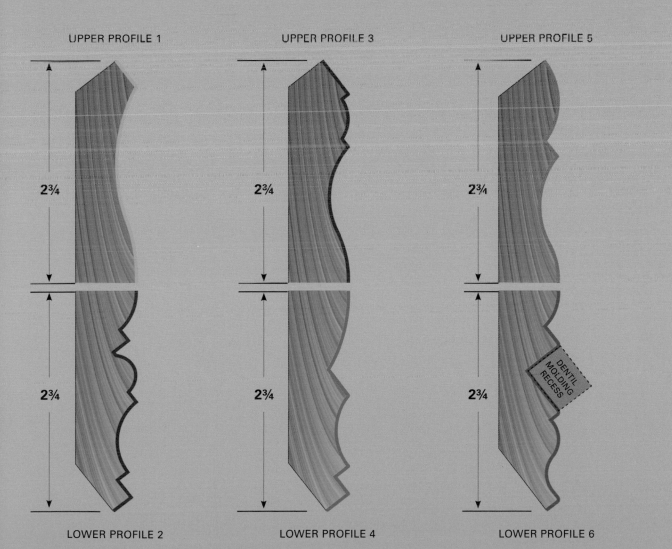

UPPER PROFILE 1

2¾

2¾

LOWER PROFILE 2

UPPER PROFILE 3

2¾

2¾

LOWER PROFILE 4

UPPER PROFILE 5

2¾

2¾

LOWER PROFILE 6

6

Beginning with the Stone Age, fire has been a source of heat. Ever since humankind moved into homes people needed to heat those homes, and the

fireplace
solutions

fireplace has answered the call. As early as the 17th century,

that source of heat and warmth has been the focal point of many

homes. Today, the fireplace still enjoys the reputation of being the

area around which furniture is gathered and the place that the

family meets at the end of the day in order to relate to one another.

If you are planning to add value to your house, it makes sense

to consider upgrading or redesigning your fireplace. And if you're

rehabbing, there's no reason that your home should not have a new

design that brings this focal area into the 21st century.

Installing a Mantle

If you're starting with an old fireplace, the first thing to look at is a fresh coat of paint, or at minimum a good cleaning. Pay extra attention to the brick or tile that surrounds the fireplace box. This area could have years of soot buildup.

If your fireplace has a rough cut timber as its mantle, replace it. Or, if you don't have a mantle at all, add one. Adding a mantle is very easy if you're starting with a simple brick façade. Pre-assembled mantles are available from home centers. For the most part mantles are hung on a wood backing that is attached to the wall.

Locate the mantle's height above the floor and center it over the firebox. Have someone hold a piece of 2×4 stock in place while you drill through the lumber using a $^1/_8$" masonry drill bit to mark the brick or tile wall behind. One hole about every 16" will do. Pull the lumber from the wall. Chuck up a $^1/_2$" masonry bit and drill the holes to a depth of 2".

There are specialized fasteners for this job, but I use a simple method. Once the holes are drilled, cut a $^1/_2$" × $^1/_2$" × 2" piece of wood and hammer the piece into the holes. Position the 2×4 lumber in place and drive 3" screws into each hole. This should secure the lumber to the wall. Nail a second layer of 2×4s to the face of that 2×4 and slide the mantle over the lumber. Fasten the mantle to the lumber with a few well concealed screws, and you're finished.

If the mantle is to be painted, do so after it's attached to the wall. For a stained piece, complete the staining prior to installation.

Start by replacing your mantle, if necessary. Then, consider the many options available, including side columns and an upper wood panel.

Building a Fireplace Surround

If you want to add more than just a mantle, a fireplace surround is the next step. This consists of a mantle supported by two legs that extend to the floor. Even though the main section is supported from below, the entire surround must be attached to the wall. Because it stretches across the wall, the simplest way is to fasten it at the wall studs. Use finish nails through the face of the surround. Set the nails and fill the holes with spackle before painting, or with matching filler if you're staining.

You can build this fireplace surround from stock lumber that's available from most home centers. Join three pieces (two legs and an apron) in a flat U-shape. Using pocket screws or a biscuit joiner can make this quick work. To determine the size of the components, start with the firebox. Establish the height and width of the box and figure at least $8\frac{1}{4}$" of space between the wood and the opening (check local building codes in your area). A standard firebox opening is about 28" tall and 36" wide. So, figure your legs will be about $52\frac{1}{2}$" apart and the bottom edge of the apron $36\frac{1}{4}$" from the hearth.

Make the legs from 1×6 stock ($5\frac{1}{4}$"). The mantle height should finish around 46" to 48" overall, so cut two legs at $45\frac{1}{2}$" in length. Use pocket screws to attach the apron, (1×8 material ($7\frac{1}{4}$")), to each leg holding the top edge down 2" from the top of the legs. The apron is cut to the correct length, so place pocket-screw holes at each end. Position the pieces and assemble the U-shaped unit. Sand

Attach the apron to the leg with pocket screws.

A few blocks placed on top of the apron keep the mantle from sagging. Attach crown moulding the strip of wood on top of the apron.

the unit and the surround parts to 180 grit before they're assembled.

Because the mantle is standard 1×6 stock, you need to build out the thickness of the support area or add extra depth to the mantle itself. This is accomplished by adding a strip of material across the entire width of the unit as built to this point. The strip needed is 1¹/₄" in width. Attach the strip with nails or screws from the back side of the unit. Hold the top edge of the strip flush with the top edge of the apron and allow it to extend over the two legs and be flush with the outside edge of each leg. Nail the crown moulding to this strip.

If you plan to use any standard mouldings (3¹/₄" crown moulding in our case), the surround needs to be wrapped back to the wall. Stacking of mouldings determines the depth of the mantle as well as how far out the edges of the mantle extend beyond the U-shaped assembly.

This surround dictates that the mantle length be 69¹/₄". The mantle piece is added to the top of the assembly. Use a router to create a decorative edge on both ends and the front edge of the mantle. Locate two pocket-screw holes in the top end of each leg and attach the mantle in position. Now affix the surround to the wall to ensure a proper fit. (It's also possible to build this surround completely at your workbench and install afterwards.)

If you plan to install the surround at this time, position a few nailer blocks (³/₄" × ³/₄" × 3"L) just under the mantle — between the mantle and the apron's top edge. Find the wall studs and attach the blocks to the underside of the mantle at each

Install the front piece of crown moulding first. Then fit the return pieces.

The completed surround can now be installed.

stud location. Stand the piece to the wall and drive screws through the blocks into the studs.

If you plan to complete the surround before installation, add a few pieces (³/₄" × 3"W × 2"L) to fit snuggly between the mantle and apron. These will support the mantle and prevent sagging.

Add the crown moulding to finish the surround. Cut and fit the long piece of crown moulding to the front of the mantle, then fit the return pieces at each end. These return pieces should fit tightly to the wall. (See chapter five.)

The surround is completed with the addition of the ¹/₄" × 1" lattice moulding that's wrapped along the inside edge of the legs and apron. The lattice adds another shadow line to the mantle and allows you to scribe to the brick or tile around the firebox. Use brad to hold the lattice in place.

Dressing Up a Mantle

Adding some additional mouldings to your fireplace surround will make it look stunning and add to its value even more. Even if you're adding character to your home just to please yourself, think of

Raising a mantle from the wall adds additional shadow lines to the design. Notice the filler pieces wrapping the interior where the mantle meets the tileworks.

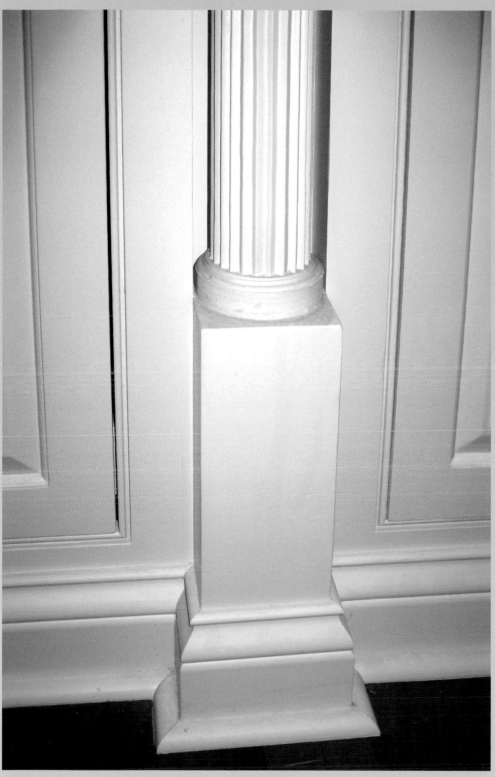

Other ideas to examine are additional mouldings used to wrap the mantle where we used the crown molding. Each additional profile adds to the shadow lines and the overall design. How about adding flutes to the face of the legs, or additional stacked pieces that are fluted with capitals to complete the column look? You can even use round columns at the fireplace mantles as shown above.

up each interior edge of the legs. These pieces fill any potential open area.

To fit this surround tight to the brick, simply use a piece of ³/₄" cove moulding, or a second piece of flat stock against the interior fill pieces.

More Ideas

Just when you think you have the surround clear in your mind, other ideas come along. What about the space above the mantle? There's no reason you shouldn't add design there as well.

Adding a paneled wall is a nice choice. Flat panels are easier to build and can be mounted flat to the wall. Raised panels require more time to complete. To make the mantle shown below, add a piece of ¼" plywood to the wall, centered over the fireplace box, and wrap pieces around all four sides flat on the wall. Rabbet these pieces so they sit on top of the plywood but still lay tight to the wall, then split the area of the panel vertically with two additional pieces that run top to bottom. Finally, wrap moulding around three sides.

If the panel is to fit tight to the ceiling, add a piece of crown moulding with returns to the wall, just as we did in the sample surround. This completes the look magnificently. If the panels don't reach the ceiling, adding a top piece or capping the unit looks great too.

Another possibility that is evident in the photo is to tie the panel above the mantle to the design of wainscot. (Building matching waincotting around the entire room will enhance the design.) Consider this if you're trying to sell a house or if you're flipping a house that you've renovated.

the time you'll spend in front of that fire, remembering the construction and enjoying the view.

One way to augment the design is to raise the entire surround off the wall and extend the project out an additional 2". In the sample surround on the previous pages, add 2"-wide strips to the back, outside edges of each leg prior to affixing the mantle to the U-shaped assembly. Doing this requires that the mantle be 2" wider. You can now use a standard 1×8 (7¹/₄") for the mantle. Also add a 2"-wide strip to the lower edge of the apron and

ALL-WOOD ROOM

If you want the design to be top-notch, look into paneling an entire wall. Incorporating the fireplace wall with built-in bookcases can make any room a thing of beauty. This process, however, is not a do-it-yourself project unless you're experienced at woodworking; it's best to leave this to a professional. But, it can add significantly to the value of your home.

A Raised Hearth

Do you have a raised hearth? Years ago, many homes had a raised brick hearth in front of the fireplace. Here are a couple of ideas for working with this feature when remodeling or updating your home. If you plan to leave the brick, simply install your mantle and surround, with or without panels above the hearth. All this means is that your mantle will be located higher above the finished floor.

But, if you want to change the hearth without tearing it from the room, cover it with tile. Tile comes in all shapes, styles and designs. Check with a tile distributor to find ways to affix the tile to the hearth.

If the hearth is in good shape, it may be as simple as adhering the tile to the brick. Another method is to cover the brick with a backer board, then add the tile.

Adding tile to a raised hearth is one way to dress it up.

This fireplace surround incorporates the entire entertainment area into the design. Small storage cupboards are installed above and below the television. Most of this project was completed with flat, simple materials available to any homeowner at home centers, but everything was arranged with great care.

7

Because old homes were built with stone and inadequate damp-proofing, they had wooden panels added to the lower portions of interior walls to act

wainscotting
and wall treatments

as insulators. This removed the chill from the dampened air and helped retain warmth in the rooms.

Today, many areas have established regulations or changed building requirements. Vapor barriers and insulation have eliminated the need of using wainscotting as insulation in homes. Now wainscotting has become a decorative element. This added trim can accentuate and enhance almost any space in your home.

Wainscotting mainly appears in foyers, living rooms and dining rooms, but it's sneaking into bathrooms and bedrooms now too. No room is off limits for this wonderful design element.

Painted (above) or stained (below) wainscotting can really dress up a room.

Install and paint the mouldings and wall with a final coat of white paint.

Paint the wall above the top moulding line with the room color, and paint below the line with white paint.

Faux Wainscot

If you want to flip a house or need a low-cost method to bring new life into your room, use these thrifty techniques to fake wainscotting..

To start, measure up from the floor and establish a level line around your room, I recommend a height lower than the normal of 36" — for this design, 28" to 30" works well.

Use any color that fits your design ideas and paint the wall above the line to the ceiling. Paint white below the line, to the top edge of the existing baseboard. One coat will do for the time being, even if it's not completely covering existing paint. (You can reverse these colors, but the majority of painted wainscotting is white. Since we are trying to fool the eye, sticking to tradition helps.)

Selecting appropriate moulding is important because it affect the whole look. To maintain a simple design, use a single chair rail. If you're looking to jazz it up a bit, stack a cap moulding on top of a flat chair rail (see illustration at right).

Locate the wall studs along the line. (I mark the studs on the underside of the line staying as close to the line as possible.) Cut and fit the base and top mouldings to the walls. Hold the top mouldings

BUILT-UP CHAIR RAIL

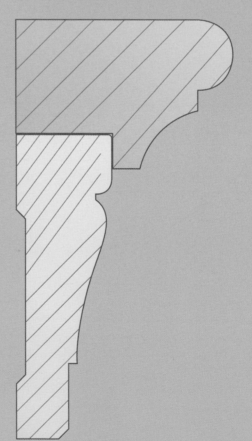

Combine two different mouldings to create a more complex and formal moulding. For example, install a chair cap moulding on top of a flat chair moulding.

above the line and attach them by driving 6d finish nails into the wall studs. Set the nails and fill the holes with spackle. (See chapter five for more information on room mouldings and their installation.)

If necessary, fill the spaces between the wall and the moulding with latex caulk. Now you're ready to paint the faux wainscot for the final time. Pull out the white paint again and add a coat to the baseboard, wall area and the newly installed chair rail. Consider using a semi-gloss paint because it makes the area appear to be one unit of wainscot.

Beadboard for that Old Farmhouse Look

Beadboard, used in a kitchen or bathroom, reminds me of a country or farmhouse look. For that reason, I favor beadboard wainscotting. Many designers use this wood paneling on ceilings for a more contemporary look.

You can buy 4 '× 8' pieces of plywood that resemble typical beadboard, or you can purchase the beadboard as individual boards or in small packs. I prefer to use the single boards and cut them to length as I'm installing them.

Typical wainscotting is the average chair rail height of 36". Installation begins as the earlier design did — with a level line drawn around the room. This eliminates the problem of non-level floors. If you begin by placing cut pieces tight to the floor, there is a distinct possibility that your finished chair rail won't be level as you round the room because your floors aren't level. I've seen this in new construction as well as remodeled houses. Take the safe route and establish the level line.

To have a finished height of 36" you need to subtract the thickness of your cap. (A cap moulding sits on top of the beadboard to cover the ends of the pieces and adds the horizontal design feature needed to balance the vertical beadboard.)

Leave a ½" gap at the bottom to account for uneven floors. Cut your boards to length, in this case, about 34½".

Use a miter saw and a stop block to accurately

cut the boards to length. Set the stop block to the left of the saw blade and allow the end of the board to rest on the block with each cut. (See photo at left.)

To accurately cut the boards to length, use a miter saw and a stop block. This ensures that all the pieces are exactly the same length.

To install the pieces on the wall, start at a door edge or window. Some carpenters like to start at the corner and work out towards a door frame or window. Either option works fine.

Glue each piece of beadboard to the wall with construction adhesive. Position the first piece, pressing it into a large S-shaped bead of adhesive. Beadboards have a tongue on one edge and a groove on the other. Install finish nails only through the tongue edge of the boards at a slight angle. (Any nail that goes in straight will inhibit the next board from sliding into position.) Use an air-powered nail gun and 1½" nails. The air gun is a dream come true. If you're nailing by hand, drill a pilot hole and use 4d finish nails.

Starting at a door edge or window, begin the installation of the beadboard pieces.

Add the second piece to the run, pressing it into the glue and fitting the groove over the tongue

Toenail the beadboards to the wall through the tongue.

Measure the last piece so it fits into the corner. Cut the piece and use a hand plane to make the fit perfect.

Attach the top cap by nailing through the cap moulding into the top ends of the beadboard panels.

of the previous piece. Nail securely when you reach a wall stud. Remember to hold the top of each piece at the level line.

When you get close to an inside corner, stop adding glue for the last few pieces, but position them in place to the run. Use a ruler or tape to get the correct width needed to complete the run. Find the widest gap between the last full-width piece and the corner. Just as the floors are not level, no corners are level or square. Rip the board to that size. You may need to plane the corner edge to get a good fit. If you have trouble fitting the pieces in the corner, remember that you can always add a piece to cover any gap.

When the last piece is fit and ready to install, add the adhesive to the wall and slide all of the pieces into position. Add a few nails at the corner where you know there's a stud.

Finish the balance of the room by repeating the adhesive, fitting the beadboards to the wall and nailing them in place. If you've held to the line accurately, the

installation of the cap should be simple. Install the top cap by nailing at each wall stud location.

Prepare the wall for paint by filling any nail holes and caulking everything tight to the wall (see chapter ten for information). Beadboard should always be painted, if not for the authentic look, then it covers up the low quality material from which it's made. Finish the installation with a couple coats of a trim paint.

Top Design

This style of wainscotting can be completed in a workshop, instead of at the building site or in the home. You can take measurements at the site and carry them into your shop to build the panels. If you do this, make sure you account for the material in the corners. If one section runs into the corner, remove that measurement from the second section in overall length.

The walls are painted with two colors. The top color will be the finished color for the room. The white of the lower section will become part of the wainscot design. Because this wainscot will be a shade of white, match that color on the lower section of the wall. If you elect to paint the wainscot a color other than white, paint the lower portion of the wall that color.

If you want to build this design but wish to finish the wainscot with a stain, replace the open areas of the design with 1/4" plywood that is the same species of wood as the trim. Matching these will ensure a similar stain finish once the work is completed.

To obtain the correct measurements, hang and case the doors prior to measuring (see chapter four for ideas). There will also be a gap of less than 3/4" at the corner junction because of the lapping of the two sections. The cap moulding will be cover this gap after the wainscot is in place.

The top color will be the finished color for the room. The white of the lower section will become part of the wainscot design.

Pocket screws are perfect for assembling the wainscot frames.

Getting Started

To begin, cut the frame pieces to size. Use a 1×6 for the end stiles, which should be the entire height of the wainscotting minus the cap moulding and the bottom rails, which will run between the end stiles. For any center stiles use a 1×8 that will fit between the top and bottom rails. If any section runs longer than eight feet, use a center stile that runs completely to the floor or mimics the end stiles. This will add support and prevent sagging in that section.

Use a pocket-screw kit to place two pocket holes at both ends of the rails and center stiles. Position the holes ³/₄" in from the edges.

Assemble the frame. I'm building a short section, so placing the center stile is relatively easy. If your section is longer you need to figure the location of each center piece. Apply the theory of the golden ratio to the proportions of the panels. (Two quantities are in the golden ratio if the ratio between the sum of those quantities and the larger one is the same as the ratio between the larger

one and the smaller. The golden ratio is approximately 1.618 and the reciprocal is .618.) Using the ratio, the width is .618 of the height. Because 35¼" is the overall height, and the space between the top of the lower rail and the bottom of the top rail is 22¼", applying the theory (22¼" × .618) would result in an open area width of 13³/₄" for each panel. This is a general rule and can be manipulated to fit your measurements.

Next, draw the layout lines for the offset of the wrap moulding (the pieces that will frame the opening). Use ¹/₄" for this measurement. You could us a combination square, but I find it easier to use a scrap of wood cut to the appropriate thickness. Position the piece at the edge of each corner and add the lines.

Cut and fit each piece of the wrap mouldings. These mouldings are 1¹/₄" in width. I couldn't find any stock mouldings at the stores to work for these pieces so I decided to make this moulding myself. (Sometimes you need to think outside the box.) The wrap moulding is made from standard chair rail which has been reduced in width. Cut the

The spacing of the stiles on a completed frame should look natural and be pleasing to the eye.

1¼" pieces with the outside edge of the chair rail against the fence of the table saw in order to create the moulding.

Next, make a 45° cut on one end of the moulding. Position the end that is mitered at one of the corners around the opening, and while holding it aligned to the next corner, mark the location of the cut. Return to the miter saw and make another 45° angle cut at that mark. Cut the first three pieces of each opening in the same manner.

Marking the length of the final piece for each opening is handled a bit differently. With one end cut to the 45° angle, position the piece with the outside or longer edge against the two adjacent angles (see photo 3). Once you align one of the

points to an existing cut, use the opposite corner to transfer the exact cut line onto the final piece of the square. Return to the miter saw and cut the piece to that mark — it should slide right into position. Make any adjustment to the length that is necessary to arrive at a tight fit.

In that same photo, you can see the reason for choosing a wider (1×8) board for the center stiles. Wrapping the openings covers 1½" of each side of the center stile. If you were to use a 1×6 for that stile you would only have 2½" of flat area between the mouldings (versus the 4¼" when using the wider board), which would make things look crowded.

Use a scrap piece of wood that is the same thickness as the offset of the wrap moulding as a template for drawing the layout lines.

Lay a piece of the wrap moulding along the layout line and mark the moulding where the perpendicular layout line intersects the moulding. This marks the inside of the 45° miter cut.

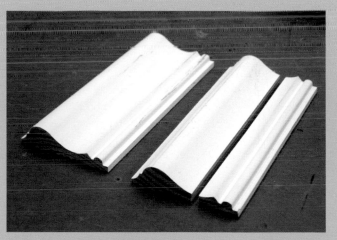

The wrap moulding is made from standard chair rail, which has been reduced in width. Rip the 1¹/₄"-wide pieces with the outside edge of the chair rail against the fence of the table saw.

Make a 45° cut on one end of the wrap moulding. Position the end that is mitered at one of the corners around the opening, and while holding it aligned to the next corner, mark the location of the cut in the mating pieces.

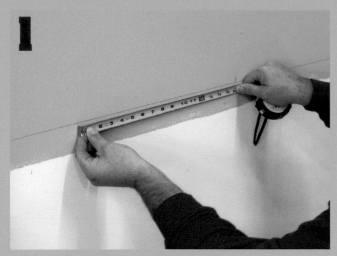

Using a stud finder, locate and mark the center of each wall stud. Make the marks above the line so they can be easily seen at installation time.

Attach the panels to the walls using trim-head screws or 2" nails. Be sure to screw into the studs!

Installation Time

Finding the studs in the wall is paramount to securing the wainscotting. Find each stud with a nail or a stud finder. Mark the center of each stud just above the line. The marks will eventually be covered with the cap mouldings. Standard stud framing is 16" on center. (Photo 1.)

Slide the wainscotting panels into position on the wall. Pull the panels tightly to any door frame and allow any discrepancy to run out in a corner (Photo 2). Remember, at the corner a second panel will butt against this panel and hide any gap. (If you have a miscalculation and the panels don't meet tightly at the corners, small gaps can be covered with a vertical moulding.) Use 1⅝" trim-head screws to attach the panels to the wall. (Trim-head

screws leave small holes that are easy to fill.) Or use 2" nails from an air-powered gun.

The next step is to use ¾" cove moulding to wrap the insides of the openings (Photo 3). This step has two purposes. First, it enhances and completes the overall look of the panels. Second, it helps pull the wainscotting tightly to the walls.

Cut the wainscot cap moulding to fit. This moulding sits on the top edge of the panels. Butt the mouldings against door openings or casings and miter them in the corners. The 45° miter cuts may need to be adjusted slightly to ensure a tight fit in each of the corners (Photo 4).

Apply two coats of trim paint to complete the work. This wainscot adds an elegant look to the room. While this system is more involved than the methods shown earlier, the effect is much richer and worth the extra effort (Photo 5).

3

After the panels have been attached to the walls, install the cove moulding.

4

This picture shows a problem that persists in most homes. With the corners of the walls not set at exactly 90°, the mouldings gap along the walls as they near these corners. Fit the miters tightly in each corner. The gaps between the top cap and the walls can be filled with latex caulk and painted to match.

5

Install the base moulding and paint the wainscotting. This is a great way to add a touch of elegance to a room.

Window seats provide a nice area in the house to relax and unwind. It is a quiet space that allows one to ponder life or enjoy a good book. Because the window

built-ins
and window seats

is the central focus, natural light plays a big part in the entire

design, but you must also have a base on which to sit.

Walk into any home center and you can find cabinets, pre-

assembled or ready-to-assemble. One thing that almost anyone

says about the shortcomings of a home is its lack of storage.

This is why I elected to combine these two subjects into one chapter. In my opinion, the best base for a window seat are cabinets, and the cabinets provide storage.

Window Seats

Window seats have a romantic notion. They suggest spare time — something that most of us don't have enough of. They're a place of personal space that allows one to connect with all that's happening indoors. The window seat can also bring a piece of the outdoors into the home by framing the window and focusing on what's on the opposite side of the glass.

Unfortunately, few homes have areas that work perfectly for a window seat. What is a perfect area? How do you know you have a good location for a window seat? The ideal position is, of course, under a window where the base of the window is at least 24" above the finished floor. To be comfortable, the seat should be around the height of a chair seat (18"). In order to get the seat in place and have the window trimmed, you'll need the 24".

This window seat is built between two walls. The front is incorporated into the walls, giving the whole thing a clean look.

The ideal location for a window seat also requires that the window be positioned between two wing walls as shown in the drawing (previous page). Then, the seat area extends from wall to wall so that a tranquil resting place is formed.

If you don't have that special area in your home, believe it or not, you can still add a window seat. You simply need to create the necessary area with other pieces of furniture or with cabinets purchased from the home center.

Let's look at a simple example of how you can accomplish this. Most bedrooms have a window that is centered or near the center of a wall.

Place a full-height bookcase or a set of base cabinets with a bookcase section above on both sides of the window, leaving space for the window seat. For a small window seat you'll need at least 42". Then, build the window seat between the two cabinets. This setup can be attached to the wall and made permanent, or it can be left free-standing as a piece of furniture that can be taken to your home. It's your call.

If you're doing extensive remodeling, another option that increases both storage and seating is to install cupboards on either side of a window. (Again, a bedroom is a great location for this scenario.)

When a window seat is created, there is a substantial amount of space left under the seat — too much space to ignore. That's valuable real estate in your home. You need to make that space useful having access under the seat.

There are actually two ideas here. One is the built-in window seat and the other is a bench located in front of the windows. The bench is a simple solution but doesn't add to the value of the house. Cat is optional.

There are two ways to access the storage area. Use a flip-top as the seat or gain entry from the front. It is a matter of personal preference.

An inexpensive way to build a window seat is to add a small wall in front of the window, spacing it at the front edge of wing walls or even with cabinetry. Cover the wall with drywall that is finished and painted. From there add a seat by nailing a frame to wall framing, then attaching a lid using a continous hinge. To finish, add a small moulding around the frame, fitted to the wall.

To dress up this window-seat area, you could use a beadboard design, add faux wainscot as shown in chapter seven or use stained hardwood for the frame and seat.

In my opinion, top access is not the best choice for the storage space because you need to remove the seat cushions or pillows in order to open the lid. Save the top access for a storage area that seldom is used for extended sitting or relaxation.

Front Access

This design looks nice and makes it easy to access the storage area, although you may have to get on your knees to do so.

To stretch your budget, you can build this seat by, again, starting with a small stud wall that fits between the wing walls. However, instead of add-

Home center stores have a plethora of door styles
from which to choose.

ing drywall, add a face frame and doors as the
front of the window seat. Build and install the face
frame, attaching it to the stud wall for support,
then install the doors.

Not interested in building doors? You can purchase doors in many sizes from the home center.
If this is your plan of attack, purchase the doors
prior to building the face frame.

Another design idea is to use cabinets for your
window seat. (Remember, I grouped window seats
and cabinets for a reason.) You will spend a few
more dollars to gain a great looking window seat,
but you will greatly reduce the amount of time and
energy required to finish the job.

The best cabinets to use are those that are generally associated with the refrigerator. A wall cabi-

net used over that appliance is usually the exact
size needed for the average window seat. Again,
check the measurements before purchasing any
cabinets. These cabinets are available in a number
of widths. The trick is to find one or a combination
of several that work for the width of the window
seat you're planning.

Because these are wall cabinets and have no
base frame or toe kick area, you need to begin
with a 2×4 frame as the base on which to set these
cabinets. This could be set back 4" from the front
edge of the cabinet front, which is the toe kick
area (the look resembles that of the standard kitch-
en base cabinet). Or, if the design calls for it, the
frame can be flush in the front. In this scenario the

For making window seats, choose 15-18"- tall wall cabinets.

façade covered by the end walls. (The bookshelves facing the window seat are a nice touch. You could use narrow cabinets like those available in broom closets, as a substitute for the bookcases.)

The look is completed with the use of small shelves over storage cupboards at the ends. Trimming the entire wall with a common baseboard and mouldings pulls the wall into a single cohesive design that adds value to any home.

If you plan to create the look of a custom-made window seat and cabinets, it's important to use mouldings, end panels and other accessories that match the cabinets. These extra items are sold separately by the cabinet manufacturer. Otherwise, your assembled units end up looking like a group of stacked boxes.

Notice the amount of storage and the front access for items under the window seat. Now, take a look at the left photo on page 95. This also qualifies for an extreme treatment in window seats.

The cherry woodwork is excellent. Only a true master carpenter and designer could tie in with the wainscot and window trim. The raised panels and the mitered sticking (the way the small moulded edge of the frame nearest the panels are matched at 45°) make this a work of art.

Another nice area for a window seat is designed into bay windows. This setting does not require you to reconstruct anything except a small wall. By adding the wall in a straight line across the room, thus separating the pushed out bay from the balance of the room, you create an area that is perfect for a window seat. Choose either top or side access for the cabinet, and finish the wall and top with the design ideas that you feel will impact your home in the best fashion. There is no better *wow* factor than to have a great sitting area with the many angles presented in a bay window setting. See right photo page 95.

framing is eventually covered by a baseboard that unites the completed grouping.

Fit the cabinets together with screws so that their face frames are tight, flush and secure so they become a single unit. Set the unit in place and attach it to the walls and/or the 2×4 base frames. Add the top and any trim mouldings to complete the window seat.

Fancy Designs

Creating a window seat between cabinets that are set into position is good, but a full-wall design is great. The photo on page 94 features a fantastic look that is accomplished with store-bought, ready-to-install cabinets and end walls that match the cabinets.

The cabinets below the double window are wall cabinets set onto a base frame. The units standing on either side of the window, forming the seat area, are bookcases set 90° to the wall, with the front

If All Else Fails

Let's say you don't have the window seat area or even a window with which to create a special nook for relaxation, and you're not into remodeling the house to create a window seat. What are you to do? I have a few ideas that will allow you to pull that look together in your home.

If you don't have anywhere to add a stack of cabinets or if the cost is prohibitive, look to the corner of a room.

The idea is the same as discussed with the bay window. Start by adding a small wall to create the window seat, but this time fit the wall across a cor-

ner of the room. Add cleats along the two full walls extending into the corner (these are for attaching the top). Finish the front with any design discussed earlier and add the top — hinged for access.

You now have a window seat without a window. It's time to allow your creativity to bloom. How about adding a mirror, or a pair of mirrors, to the wall for increased light? Maybe you have a bit of artistic flair and can paint the window onto the wall.

The addition of a window casing (see chapter four) and possibly a sill brings the look that much closer to reality. Add a few soft pillows and you have a great area for your trip into relaxation.

This wall of storage cabinets, open bookcases and window seat was made using off-the-rack kitchen cabinets and mouldings.

Stained-wood adds warmth to a room.

A bay window is a perfect location for a window seat.

Words of Wisdom

With any construction project such as a window seat, there are a few pieces of wisdom to learn.

If you examine the windows in your home or rental house you'll notice that the floor vents are located in the same vicinity as the windows. It always happens that way. You must make amends to keep these areas in working order. That can sometimes mean calling a professional to relocate any heating and cooling runs. Or, you can extend the ductwork to the front of the seat. Try to locate a vent in the toe kick area and keep as much storage space available as possible.

flip tip

Some building codes require that the windows near a window seat include safety glass. Always check local building codes before starting a project of this type.

As you move into a house or start reno-vating rental property, there are many small things that you can do to help bring the property back from disrepair.

repair
and replace

These are simple fixes that seem so easy after you think about it, but at the time, never enter your thoughts. I cover both repair tips and kitchen cabinet doors in this chapter.

Windows with plastic jambs can sometimes be pushed enough to break them loose if they've been shut.

Windows that Don't Open

While being cooped up in the house during the winter months, you broke down and put a fresh coat of paint on the wood trim. Now that the air is warm enough to crack open the windows and enjoy the freshness, the windows don't budge. You've painted them shut.

Nothing is more frustrating than not being able to open the windows. Pounding on the window could be the right thing to do, but you may be using the wrong technique.

If your windows are of a fairly new design, meaning the entire sash can be removed, start by pushing on the jamb. Chances are it is a plastic material that moves as you apply pressure. This could be all it takes to produce the desired result. If this doesn't work or your windows aren't new, read on.

Your next option is to use a utility knife (bottom left photo) to trace along the edge where the painted surfaces touch. You may need to repeat the cut several times to free the unit, but if it is lightly stuck this should do the trick.

No luck? Now it's time to move to the heavy artillery, but don't use your fist. Pounding with your fist only affects the window in a small area. Unless you actually hit the correct point at the beginning, your hand will become quite sore before you free the window.

Instead, grab a piece of 2×4 lumber about 10 – 12" long, place it alongside the frame, and tap the lumber with a hammer (lower photo). This sends the jolt along the entire length of lumber so you cover more ground in less time and reduce the chance of damaging your hand or the glass. If this doesn't work, you must have nailed the window shut!

So, how do you avoid this in the future? Simple — remember to operate the window a time or two as the paint dries — winter cold or not.

Broken Glass Fixes

There are two major types of broken glass. The first is when the neighbor kids send a baseball into the window. Crack. It's time to replace the glass. The second is when you notice a film or cloudiness to your double-pane glass. This may be slow to show up and indicates a broken seal or air leak between the panes of glass.

If your windows have single-pane glass, the fix is simple. Spend the time to remove the old putty around the pane, carefully remove the broken glass,

Window glazing, painter's putty and a putty knife are all you need to install, reinstall or reseal windows.

Double paned windows have two reflections.

then buy a replacement piece at the local hardware store. Don't forget to pick up new glazing putty.

Installation is a reverse process. Position the glass into the spot, use a few glass points (pick these up at the hardware store also) to hold it in place and apply the putty around the perimeter of the pane with your fingers. Once the putty is evenly applied, use the putty knife to smooth the surface of the putty.

But, if you have double-pane glass the job is not a do-it-yourself fix. How do you know if you have double-pane glass? Hold a flame up to the window. If you see two flames in the glass you have double-pane, sometimes called insulated, glass.

Remove the entire window sash and take it to a glazer in your area. They will be able to fix the unit.

Doors that Stick

In chapter three we looked at a few quick fixes for doors that sag or stick, then moved on to replacing the unit. If the door is wooden there is another option — using a hand plane to fit the door to the frame.

Begin by trying the quick fixes suggested in chapter three. These need to be completed before you move on anyway. If you correct a door using the plane and then pull the hinges tight as suggested in the earlier chapter, the newly fitted door will have unsightly gaps. Working in the correct order is a must.

If you've reached the point when you need to work on the door slab to make it fit, begin by closing the door in the jamb. Grab a compass scribe and set the distance to the widest gap on the knob side of the door. Do this by placing the metal tip of the scribe against the door casing and setting the pencil portion to the edge of the door.

Next, tighten the scribe or hold the tool tight to keep it from moving as you trace the line at the edge of the door slab. As you move along the door's edge, keep the metal point of the scribe tight to the casing edge. The pencil line is the line to which you must plane.

Use a standard compass to scribe an ill-fitting door to its frame.

Remove the door from its hinges. It's best to remove the hinge pins instead of the screws. If you cannot get a screwdriver below the cap of the pin to gently pry the pin upward, use a nail set and and a hammer. Tap the nail set with the hammer (shown at right) until the pin moves up, then finish the job with the screwdriver.

Place the door with the hinge side toward the floor. Have someone hold the door or find a way to clamp the slab so it will not move as you plane.

If the door is made of pressed hardboard, you can immediately begin planing the edge to the pencil line. However, if the door is truly wood, you need to examine the wood grain to determine the direction you need to plane. If you move the plane in the wrong direction the cut will be difficult. Stop and change your direction. You should notice a difference in the cutting action.

I like the low angle block plane for this job. Set the blade for a shallow cut, removing a shaving at a time. Trying to remove too much wood with a single cut makes the job much harder.

Work to the line, making the last pass along the corner to slightly round the edge. Hang the door back in the frame by replacing the hinge pins. The fit should be good and the door should now swing freely. A final touch with 120-grit sandpaper, and the freshly exposed edge is ready for finish.

Changing Doorknobs

A non-operating doorknob is a nuisance. Whether it's an interior door or and exterior door, if the knob doesn't turn, you don't gain access to the room or the house. You can try blowing a small

A low angle block plane is the perfect tool for fitting a wooden door.

amount of powdered graphite into an entry doorknob where a key is involved, but you will probably have to change the doorknob anyway. They are not made to last forever. Also, if this is a rental house you should change the knobs for security reasons.

To change the passage (for egress only) or privacy (includes a locking mechanism) doorknob on an interior door, begin by removing the two screws on the cover from one side of the door. As the screws release, that part of the knob is removed. Push the latch in at the door's edge to remove the second half of the knob (photo 1). Complete the

Egress doorknob replacement parts come as a complete set that you can find at the local home center.

outside of the doors. If the knob should fail, gaining access to the screws makes replacement much easier.) Line up the spindle (the half round post permanently attached to the knob) with the holes in the latch. Remember to depress the latch to allow the spindle to slide into position.

Next, slide the screws portion of the knob into position. As you do this, you need to align the center of the knob in a certain position to ensure that the parts fit together. If this is a privacy knob there is a small oval rod inside the spindle that has to be positioned correctly as well. Once the knob slides tight to the door, the fun begins.

The long screws that hold the knob halves together can be difficult to start. Place one of the screws into the hole and pull the knob away from the door as far as possible without disconnecting the union. You should be able to see the hole that the screw fits into in order to make the connection. Get the threads locked on that screw, then start the second screw using the same method (photo 2).

After both screws are started, tighten them together. You cannot wind one screw completely before turning the other. If you turn one in a long way before turning the other, it's much harder to gain access to the second screw.

All doorknobs are installed in approximately the same way. Understanding the basic process is key to replacing most any doorknob.

removal by pulling the screws that hold the latch in the door's edge. Using a screwdriver, remove the two screws that are 3/4" in length.

To install a new knob, you need to reverse the process. But, there are a few quirks that need to be addressed first. After you install the latch with the necessary screws, position the spindle portion of the knob to the latch. Be sure to install the doorknob appropriately. That is, position the locking mechanism for a privacy lock on the inside of the room that is to be secured. (I also make sure the screws on a passage knob are positioned on the

Kitchen Cabinet Doors

Most kitchen repairs are done to the cabinets. Either the doors or drawers are in need of attention. Generally, I see broken or misaligned door hinges or drawer fronts that are not properly connected. These fixes are straightforward.

Replace the hinges. Good replacement hinges are available at your local hardware store. remember to take a prototype with you. Install the necessary new hardware, and you're done.

Fixing the drawer front can be simple as well. It may be a matter of adding a few extra screws through the inside of the drawer box to hold the drawer front in position. Rehabbing the drawers is more complex if the drawer box is broken. You need to replace the box by removing the drawer glides. If the front face is attached, save it for later use. Build or buy a new drawer box, reinstall the front face and hardware, and fit the new drawer back into the cabinet.

The biggest difference you can make in your home or investment property is to spruce up those kitchen cabinets. It's easy to allow the spending to get out of control. So, what can you do to update the cabinets without a full replacement? The simple answer is to paint. The answer that leads to more work and/or expense is to replace the doors and drawer fronts.

To paint the cabinets, it's necessary to clean all surfaces. Any grease left on the surface will repel paint and cause further problems. Once the clean-ing is complete and dry, scuff the surface with 120-grit sandpaper. Apply a primer coat, then a final coat of washable latex. Or better yet, use two coats of acrylic or oil-base paint.

Resurfacing the cabinets is a job for a professional or an aggressive home woodworker. Whether you choose to pay the professional or tackle the job yourself, the cabinet doors and drawer fronts must be replaced and the surface of any exposed areas must be covered in matching material to complete the transformation.

If you bypass the professionals, start the process with a trip to the home center. They have literature that explains the process and helps you get accurate measurements for ordering purposes. The selection is vast. It will take time to arrive at a decision and will take about three weeks to get the cabinet parts shipped in. I suggest researching these two scenarios closely before deciding on a course of action.

European hardware like the door hinges shown here, drawer fronts and slides (left) and doors (below) are all available at your local home center.

Neither preparing for the finishing steps nor the actual finishing is part of the trim carpenter's assignment. But, if you need to do that work, this is a short guide.

preparation
and finish

If you understand the concepts in this chapter, you'll have fewer

hassles and better prices when paying someone to do this work.

The major decision in trim carpentry is whether you are paint-

ing or staining the finish. This is big is because the choice deter-

mines the order of the work. If you plan to stain the woodwork, the

staining and top coats need to be applied prior to installation. If, on the other hand, you plan to paint the finished woodwork, you can install the trim prior to painting the final coat.

In either case, paint the walls with a first coat before starting the trim work. In the years that I've done trim carpentry, and in all the years my father built homes, I never once used a wall primer. I always start with new drywall surfaces and add the first coat of regular latex paint as the primer. Primer is only necessary if you have walls that are stained with something that repels paint (see flip tip). It is not needed to hold the topcoat of paint to the wall.

Let's walk through each scenario. I suggest purchasing trim and mouldings in bulk lengths (they have to be stainable surfaces). Apply stain and two layers of top coat prior to starting the trim work. Cut, fit and install all the trim throughout the rooms or the entire house. Next, go back and paint the walls with a second coat. This requires that you make the joints and areas that fit to the walls very tight so no gaps show. Be careful when painting near the edges of the trim, or mask the edges of the trim.

Get Ready to Paint

If you are painting the woodwork, purchase primed trim and mouldings for your renovation. It's less expensive and has already been primed, which means you can immediately start the carpentry work. With any material that is not primed, cut the pieces to length and prime them with a single coat of latex paint prior to installation. Cut and fit the mouldings in any manner discussed throughout this book. You should always do the best work possible, but if you have an area that just doesn't fit as nicely as you had hoped, don't fret.

Once the trim work is complete and before you think about painting, it's time to hide any flaws. Start by filling the nail holes (I like to use window glazing compound) left from attaching the trim to the walls. Next, take a look at the flat corners of the door casing. If you haven't achieved the optimal fit, use a small amount of latex caulking at the intersection of the two pieces. Push the caulk into the crack and smooth the surface with your finger.

Next, look at the top edges of the baseboards or along the door casings. Use latex caulking to fill any gaps. Run a small bead along the edges — I run every length to assure a tight look — rubbing it in and smoothing the area with your finger. This might seem like a long process, but I assure you that the results are worth the effort. Now you're ready to apply the final coat of paint.

flip tip

If you have a spot that bleeds or seeps through paint, use a coat of shellac (bought from the hardware store) between the spot and your topcoat. The shellac seals the area and the paint easily covers the shellac.

Use caulk to fill any gaps between the walls and trim. Use painter's putty to fill nail holes.

Because you fill gaps with caulk, your walls flow seamlessly into the mouldings you have installed when the final painting is finished.

Paint edgers are the best and easiest way to paint into corners and around trim.

Painting the Final Coat

With the caulking completed, you can start applying the final coats of paint. I'll give you the steps for achieving a first-class finish. You can also apply these techniques to the first coat of wall paint before the trim is installed.

Get out your paint pan, roller and edger. (The ceiling should be finish painted prior to beginning the walls.)

Paint all inside corners. Apply the paint with a 2" brush so the corners are covered and the paint extends away from the corner about 2". Apply paint along the top edge of the wall where the wall and ceiling meet.

The paint edger is going to make you wonder how you have gotten along without this tool for so long. It makes painting the top edge of the wall without getting anything on the ceiling a snap. To load the edger, first load the roller. Take the loaded roller and run it along the pad of the edger as if you're painting the tool. Climb the ladder so you can reach the intersection and position the edge with the wheels tight to the ceiling. Roll the edger along the ceiling as the paint glides onto the wall surface. Keep the wheels clean, and the painting task is over in no time.

Next trim around the door and window casings. Use a brush to cut in and run the paint over the caulked portions of the trim. I usually paint down onto the baseboards and onto any casings to make sure I get a coat of paint onto these areas. Don't worry about the wall paint on the trim. It will be covered when the trim is painted.

Using roller pan liners makes for easy cleanup. Simply discard them when you're finished.

Rolling the Paint onto the Walls

Now you're ready to paint the walls. There's a secret to this work. Load the roller from the pan. A roller extension is nice to make reaching high up on the ceiling and the walls easier — no ladder required. Roll paint onto the walls away from the corner and paint only the top half of the wall. As you roll on the paint, work back tight to the corner, then move across the wall.

When the paint gets thin, load the roller again. Contact the wall away from where you just finished and move back to lap the previous coverage. Slowly move across the wall. Each time you load the roller, repeat these steps.

After you've coated about six feet of wall, move to the bottom half of the wall and use the same technique to paint there. Before loading the roller for another go-round, move to the first completed area, then swoop into the wall about a third of the way up, roll over the paint joint between the top half and bottom half of the wall, and pull away as

you reach the area about a third of the way from the top of the wall. This is to cover any lapping of paint. It blends the painted joint line and hides the joint from eye level.

Painting the Woodwork

With the walls painted, it's time to add the final touch to the trim and mouldings. I suggest using a satin sheen for the trim. Unlike the flat wall paint, the higher sheen allows the trim to stand out when painted and it is easier to clean. This is my personal preference so you should adjust the sheens to your desire.

Be careful when painting the trim. You want to paint the baseboard and casings without getting paint on the wall surfaces. You can pay attention and do this work by hand or use blue painter's tape to mask the walls where they meet the trim.

With pre-primed trim you may be able to get by with a single coat of paint, but figure on two to be on the safe side. This completes the painting job. For more in-depth painting ideas and details, consult with a professional or look into specialized books.

flip tip

If you're painting the room without painting the trim, an edger works great for painting next to the trim around the door and window casings.

Any house looks better with hardwood floors. They add warmth to a house that carpet, vinyl flooring or ceramic tile cannot match.

hardwood
floors

Carpet is a particularly good choice for bedrooms. But, enjoy

hardwood floors in great rooms, living rooms and dining rooms.

Starting with a great floor allows you to personalize these

rooms with your individual tastes. Adding an area rug in front

of the fireplace with seating for that intimate gathering still

maintains the warm feeling. Change the decorating scheme with

different wall colors. With carpet, even neutral colored carpet,

redecorating becomes a much harder task.

It's easy to keep wooden floors clean with a vacuum and a damp cloth. (Pulling dirt from the carpet is a daunting chore.) Hardwood floors are multi-purpose and don't wear out. Worn carpet can be found in most homes.

Whether you're changing the carpet in your house or you're flipping a house, there are lots of wood flooring choices. Products are available that take a few days or a few hours to install. There are limitless colors, tones and designs. A professional can install the wood flooring or you can jump into the do-it-yourself club and install it yourself.

You need to spend time planning and thinking about the look you want have when the task is finished. Ask the knowledgeable salespeople for information and tips.

Caring for Hardwood

Wood floors provide a higher resale value if they are in good condition. Hardwood floors require less maintenance than other flooring choices. They simply need routine upkeep.

There are simple rules for keeping hardwood floors in tip-top shape — no matter that the finish. First, sweeping or vacuuming the floors is the most important step to maintaining great wood floors. Walking on that dust or grit destroys the finish and the wood floor.

Second, keeping the floors looking great by using mats at entrance doors. When someone enters your house, small particles and pebbles come along for the ride. Using mats captures the grit and dirt before it gets on the hardwood.

Third, area rugs keep the high traffic areas from becoming run down. Place an area rug in front of seating areas, where your dog enjoys pacing back and forth while watching the neighbor's cat and in the high-use areas of the kitchen and hallways. The rugs catch dirt before it gets to the wood floors.

Fourth, if you move furniture around your home, I'm sure you're familiar with floor protector pads. These pads are made from felt or soft carpet pieces and are positioned under furniture feet and legs. Sliding the heavy furniture along the wood floors can be damaging if the ends of the feet aren't covered. It takes one tiny stone to instantly damage hardwood beyond a simple repair. Keep protector pads clean and free from dirt.

Clean the wood floor by sweeping or vacuuming.

Restore the luster to a wood floor with a coat of boiled linseed oil.

Fifth, keep the tips or the heels of your shoes clean. Grit, dirt, mud and small rocks can scuff and dents floors. When working with wax finishes, follow the manufacturer's guidelines for caring for your floor.

For oil and/or wax finished floors there are a few things to know. Never use water-based cleaners on oil/wax finished wood floors. Water seeps into the cracks and crevices of the floor and settles in for the long haul. The wood rots and the mildew and/or mold can stain the area, adding dark, almost black, spots to the floors.

After removing dust or dirt by sweeping or vacuuming, you may notice the floor has lost its luster. On a waxed floor, the sheen can be renewed by buffing with a dry soft cloth — cotton works great. It's either hands-and-knees time or wrap the cloth over a dust mop. If that doesn't restore the luster, try adding additional paste wax, especially in high traffic areas. But, don't over-wax the floor.

Clean up any spills immediately with a damp a cloth, and buff dry with a second cloth. If one of these spills goes undetected, in a short period of time, you'll see a white ring or spot. Fix this with

No.0000 steel wool and a small amount of mineral spirits, Rub the area in small circles until the white spot has vanished. Then, after the area is completely dry, apply a coat of paste wax and buff.

Film Finishes

Film finishes (polyurethane) aren't very different from wax-finished floors. Follow the manufacturer's directions for cleaning, but if those guidelines aren't available, don't use a cleaner that will leave a residue (some warranties are voided if the wrong product is used). Don't soak the floor with water, and clean spills immediately. Also, it's not a good idea to wax floors finished with polyurethane because they will become very slippery.

Finding the Mother Load

In the Midwest, during the late 1950s and throughout the early 1970s, it was common to see homebuilders installing strip-oak flooring as a subfloor

Carefully remove the carpet tack strips. Fill the tack holes with colored putty sticks.

Use colored putty sticks, scratch remover pens and crayons to repair holes and scratches.

— over which wall-to-wall carpeting was installed. It's a find to discover one of these dwellings. If you decide to expose the hardwood, rip up the carpeting and the floor is ready for a good cleaning, patching or refinishing. However, keep in mind that the carpet is the only layer protecting the room from whatever is below it. If a cold, unheated garage is below, you might find a cold morning in the middle of winter.

When the carpet extricated, you'll need to decide if the wood floor can be saved or if it requires refinishing. If the floor is unfinished or is finished, follow the steps below.

Check the floor for damage. The nail holes from the carpet tack strip are minor fixes. You're looking for major problems, for example, animal urine. If you see black spots, refinish the floor.

Look for is structural damage such as broken or heavily dented boards. These require replacement of boards and matching might be difficult if there is no extra flooring available. After replacement boards are installed the floor will need refinishing.

Fix the small dents and dings with putty sticks — available from your local hardware store or home center — that match the color of the floor. Crayons can also be used. It's a quick repair and is similar to the coloring you did in your younger days. Clean the area well and grab the stick that matches, then scribble back and forth across the scratch until the dent is filled. Then rub over the filled scratch until the spot is leveled to the floor.

Repairing the Floor

If there are major problems that cannot be fixed with sanding, for example, boards that are cracked, pieces that are warped, problems from water damage, these should be replaced. Replace boards by cutting out the damaged ones and installing new ones.

Installing replacement boards should be done with care. The last thing you want to do is damage additional pieces while repairing the bad boards. Begin by cutting a 1"-wide strip in the center of the board that is to be replaced. Pulling the 1" material from the floor allows access to the edges of the flooring. Remember, the flooring is made of

REPLACING A FLOORBOARD

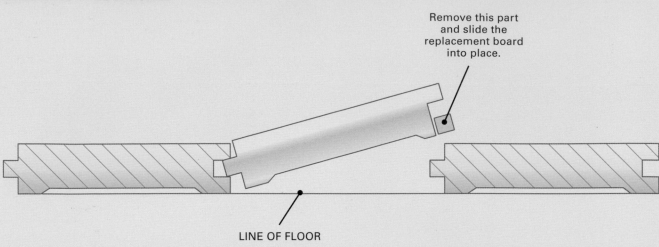

Remove this part
and slide the
replacement board
into place.

LINE OF FLOOR

tongue-and-groove pieces that are nailed to the sub-floor. Hitting a nail with your saw blade and watching the sparks fly is not an inviting scenario.

Once the cuts are made in the center of the board (cut as closely to the end of a board as possible, then finish the work with a chisel), cut across the ends of the pieces with a router or jigsaw. Remember to stagger the ends of the boards (no two boards, placed side-by-side, should end at the same point). Close attention is needed to ensure that you don't damage other boards.

Remove the center pieces and pry the outer edges away from the neighboring boards. The nails can be tricky to remove, so take your time.

You're wondering how to install the new piece and keep the groove edge intact, right? The bottom edge of the groove has to be cut away (see illustration). A table saw is the best tool for this job, but you could use a router and router table. After the edge is removed, finagle the new piece into position.

First, check the replacement board to guarantee that it will fit. It may be necessary to adjust the width of the board before installation.

Install the new piece by positioning the tongue into the groove of the neighboring piece. Tap the board to set the tongue. As you drive the board

Before installing a replacement floorboard, the bottom of the grooved edge will need to be removed.

into the grooved edge of the neighboring piece, the replacement piece will snap into the open area.

Face-nail the board to the floor with a 6d finish nail driven into the floor joist. Set the nail head below the surface before sanding.

Refinishing the Floor

After the floor has been repaired, it can be refinished. The first operation has nothing to do with the actual floor. It begins at the tool rental store. Pick up a floor sander, floor edge-sander, a pad sander and a floor buffer. And, don't forget the appropriate sanding pads, discs and sheets.

An edger sander is used to sand the floor next to the walls.

Remember to pickup sanding discs and belts from the tool rental store.

You'll need sanding belts for the floor sander and discs for the edge sander that are 36, 50 and 100 grit. Pick up sheets of sandpaper for the pad sander in 120 grit as well as larger discs for the floor buffer in 150 grit. Ask the rental store clerk to help with the quantities of each. With these tools and accessories in hand, it's time to start working on the floor.

If you're refinishing the floor in a single room, add sheets of plastic to the doorways to reduce the amount of dust traveling into other parts of the house. Remove furniture from the area and remove the shoe-moulding strip from the baseboards.

Set up the floor sander with a 36-grit sanding belt. Start sanding in the middle of the room and move towards the wall, working in the direction of the grain. Sand half the room.

Sand the second half of the room, starting in the middle of the room and working towards the wall. Overlap any previously sanded areas. Do not allow the sander to cut a trough at the center of the room. Sand the balance of the room. Resand pet stains if necessary. They should disappear completely while sanding. Fan out the sanded area so as not to have a divot or depression appear in the floor.

After the major area of the floor sanded, it's time use the edge sander. Begin with 36-grit sandpaper sand the edges of the floor at the wall. Keep this tool in constant motion or tilt the disc off the floor while stopped. (Holding it in one spot will sand dips in the floor.) Work completely around the room until the balance of the old finish is removed.

Fill in the cracks, crevices at the ends of the boards and nail holes with solvent-based wood filler. (Some of these products are made with wood, so they stain like real wood.) Do not fill the gaps between the boards. Filler forced into these gaps will impede the natural movement of the floor as it expands and contracts during the seasons. Use solvent-based fillers with adequate ventilation, and follow the printed safety precautions.

Return to the floor sander and sand the floor as you did earlier, this time using a 50-grit sanding belt. Use the 100-grit for the last pass with this machine. Follow-up the floor sander with the edger, working through the 50- and 100-grit discs.

Getting into a square corner is impossible using a round sander. A paint scraper will easily romove the old finish.

Scraping in the direction of the grain with a hand scraper, remove the old finish from the inside corners of the room.

Finish sand the floor around the perimeter of the room with the pad sander using 120-grit sandpaper. This removes heavier scratches left by the edge sander

Use the buffer with 150-grit sanding discs to erase the heavy scratches left by the floor sander. You could use the buffer for the entire job but it would take longer than using the floor sander.

You're almost there. Vacuum the floor before applying the stain. If you leave sanding dust on the floor to be gathered into the stain, you've wasted time getting the floor level, stripped and ready to finish. Vacuum the floor slowly to catch as much dust as possible.

How About That Stain?

The time has come and you're ready to stain the floor. Choose the color carefully because it's a big decision. I've seen professional floor refinishers bring in six or more sample colors for customers to help them in their decision process. After removing

Use an orbital sander to sand into corners and remove the sanding marks left by the edge sander.

Use wood filler, colored to match your wood floor, to fill in the end joints between the floor boards and any nail holes.

A floor buffer will accept sandpaper and is used to final sand a wood floor.

the old finish and prior to sanding with the 100-grit belts, try a few colors on scraps or on the floor. You can see the color on the floor and then sand the samples away as you prepare the floor.

You'll need the well-mixed stain in gallon cans, a handful of cotton cloths to apply and wipe the stain and a pair of rubber gloves that are heavy enough to withstand the solvents in the stain. (Stick with the solvent-based stains because they don't raise the wood's grain and they dry slowly.) Also, use eye protection. There's no sense taking any chances.

Staining begins with a soaked rag and applying the stain to the floor, working about 12" of floor with each pass. Keep a wet edge as you move across the floor, working from one side of the room to the other. Wipe the stain on, then use a dry cloth to wipe away any excess and to even the color and tone of the floor. When the first 12" is stained, move to the second and work from wall to wall. Continue until the floor has been stained. Allow the stain to dry for 24 hours.

If you used a solvent-based stain, you can start applying the finish coats when the stain is dry. If you used a water-based stain, you may need to lightly sand the floor to remove any fibers or fuzzies that appeared due to the water. This is done by hand sanding using 400-grit sandpaper or an equivalent disc on the buffer. If you use the buffer, be careful not to sand through the stain and into the wood.

Before final sanding, test different stains to see which one you like. These stains can then be sanded away. Wear eye protection when using stains. Some stain fumes can irritate your eyes.

Topping it Off

The first coat of polyurethane acts as a sealer to the stain. Apply this as well as subsequent topcoats in the same manner. Professionals use a special paint roller applicator made of lamb's wool with a short nap to spread the polyurethane. Load the finish into the applicator and roll the floor like painting a wall. Apply the topcoat like you stained the floor, by working in a 12" section and moving from wall to wall before advancing to the next section. Allow the polyurethane to dry.

When the first coat is dry, sand the edges by hand with 120-grit sandpaper. Use the buffer with 150-grit, but go at it easy. All you're doing is knocking off any nibs (high spots) left in the finish. Vacuum the floor and apply another coat of polyurethane. Two coats should do the job, but a third could be added for extra protection.

So You Want a New Floor.

What do you do if you weren't lucky enough to find hardwood floors under your worn out carpet, but you want the warmth and look of wood? Decide what type of flooring you like and look into a new installation of hardwood flooring.

flip tip

Decide if you want a high sheen like a gymnasium floor, or something more subdued that looks as if there is no finish on the floor. You can find these and all sheens inbetween at your local home center.

Plank flooring is available in two thicknesses, $1/2$" and $3/4$". The widths are varied with this type of flooring. Standard sizes range from 3" to 8". Custom designs can be wider. Installations of this floor mix the widths. This type and the strip version of hardwood floors are installed the same way, with additional steps because of the varying plank widths.

These floors are also available pre-finished. The installation is the same but the finishing step is eliminated. Usually the edges of the boards are beveled to hide slight imperfections in the heights of the boards.

Strip flooring ranges in thicknesses from $5/16$" to $3/4$" and is available in widths of $1^1/2$", 2" and $2^1/4$". The $2^1/4$"-flooring is standard. The same width pieces are used throughout the room. This type of floor is installed, sanded and finished in the home. It can be re-sanded and refinished several times throughout its life.

Engineered flooring is made in layers similar to plywood, with the top layer being hardwood. This top layer can vary in thickness, the thickest of which can be refinished.

There are four types of hardwood flooring. Don't confuse *types* of flooring with *different hardwoods*. Three types are shown at left.

The other type is *parquet flooring*. It's made of individual wood slats arranged in many different geometrical patterns and the pieces are held together by mechanical fasteners. Thicknesses range from 1/4" to 1/2". The flooring is installed with adhesive.

Other Choices

Laminate flooring (photo above) is sandwich constructed. There is a backing material, usually a melamine laminate, set with a second layer of a high-quality photographic paper or real wood veneer and a top layer of melamine laminate for protection.

Laminate flooring floats on the sub floor. The floors are assembled into a floating sheet of flooring, individual pieces are glued and snapped together to form the panel.

Which floor should you choose? Laminate or natural wood — each has its pros and cons. If you scratch a hardwood floor, you can fix the scratch, as talked about earlier, with fillers or completely refinish the floor.

Scratch a laminate floor and the fix is not so easy. Small scratches can be filled, but refinishing

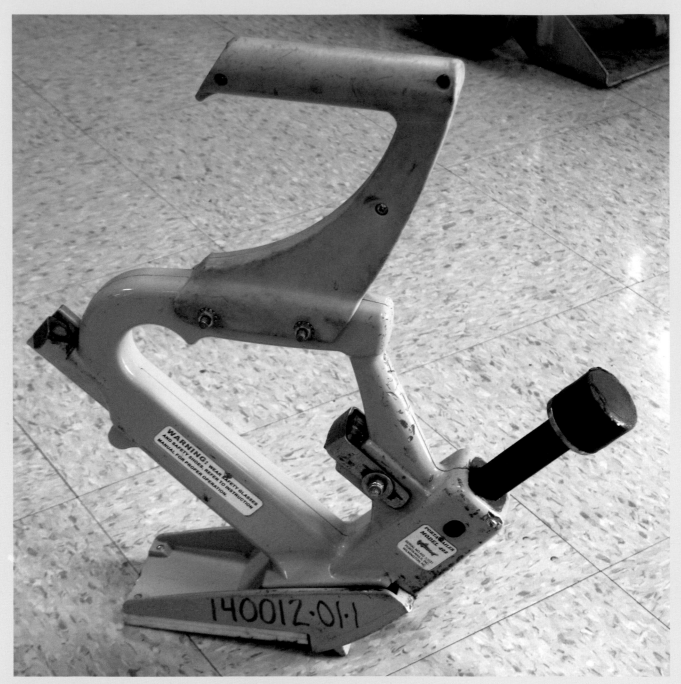

A floor nailer makes installing tongue-and-groove floor boards easy. The tool fits in the space above the tongue. A good whack with a heavy mallet on the piston will install the nail at a 45° angle into the board. When then next board is installed, the nail will be hidden.

the laminate floor is out of the question because there's no wood to refinish.

A benefit of laminate over hardwood is the finish. Laminate floors won't fade in the sun or age with a yellowing cast. These floors don't need to be waxed and if water is left sitting in a puddle overnight or longer, you'll find no discoloration or white rings to deal with. This is not to say that laminate floors are impervious to water — just that it takes a lot to create a problem.

Installation: Ready, Set, Go

Installing a floor is a big job that can be completed by a homeowner with time and patience. You can

An air-powered floor nailer does the same thing as a standard floor nailer, but it does it will a lot less work on your part. And it does it lots faster.

make the room sing with that warm feeling of hardwood. Strip flooring and plank flooring are installed using similar methods. I'll describe the installation for the strip flooring and note variations in the plank flooring as necessary

Bring the flooring into the home or room where it is to be installed. All wood has moisture and needs to acclimate to its surrounding. The process is ongoing — if the humidity is high the wood will gain moisture and if the humidity is low the wood loses moisture.

If you were to store the flooring in the basement of your house (higher humidity), then bring it up to the next level and start installing immediately, the boards would twist and move, causing problems with the pieces already installed, as they acclimated to their new surroundings. Allowing the flooring to acclimate helps with the installation and the finished results are much better. Note: Wood floors will move. Small gaps can show between the boards during winter months, and will disappear as the humidity levels increase during the summer months.

Getting the Right Tools

Before you begin laying the new floor, you'll need to gather the tools for the job. Most of the tools you should have on hand. There are a couple tools that you'll probable neet to rent.

If you're a handy do-it-yourself homeowner, you should have a saw to cut the flooring. Don't try to use a handsaw for this job. Your arms will be tired enough from nailing the floor in place. Use a miter saw (as described in chapter one). A miter saw cuts squarely and is safe if used properly. If you do not have a miter saw, you can use a circular saw and a combination square as a guide. The cut might not look as good depending on your sawing abilities, but most of the cuts are at the ends near the walls and will be covered with baseboard or shoe moulding.

Drill a counterbore hole into the pieces down to the floor joist. This hole allows you to install the screw and have room left to add a plug to cover the screw head.

Let's look at a floor nailer. You can handnail this flooring if you have a few pieces to install, for example, a small bathroom of no more than twenty-five square feet (a five-foot square area). Anything bigger, rent a nailer.

There are two types of floor nailers. One is hammer actuated and the blow drives the nail. The other is also hammer actuated but compressed air drives the nail. Choose one based on the availabil-ity of a compressor and on the amount of flooring you install. The bigger job dictates the air-powered tool. (Don't forget to pick up nails for the nail-ers.) The rental store clerk will get you the correct amount of nails based on your total square footage of floor to be installed, so take the room and floor-ing information with you to the store.

You need a battery- or electric-powered drill, a pry bar, a tape measure, a hammer, No.30 roofing

Make a plug from matching flooring with a plug cutter and your drill, or purchase plugs. Add glue to the plugs and tap them into the holes.

felt, a dust mask, a chalk line and safety glasses. If you decide to hide any face attaching devices (nails or screws), you'll need a counterbore and plug cutter.

Installing the Wood Floor

There are rules to follow when installing wood floors. Floors are installed perpendicular to the floor joists. Locate the joists in your room and mark them. You might have to install flooring parallel to the joints if the joists change direction (a structural building thing). Leave a $1/2$" to $3/4$" gap

(follow the manufacturer's guidelines) around the perimeter of the room. No two ends of boards should finish at the same point in the floor. Stagger the ends of the individual pieces a minimum of 6" — 12" or more is best.

Establish guidelines for the installation by finding the center of each wall. Snap a chalk line between opposite walls, forming a cross in the middle of the room. Measure from one snapped line to a wall to establish a straight starting point. Select the straightest flooring pieces available and lay them out near the starting wall. Check the pieces for damage and blemished cuts. About five percent of the flooring will have problems, gener-

Sand the plugs flush before finishing the floor.

ally at the ends of the boards because they're not cut square. Cut an end squarely and use it as a starting piece or an ending piece in one of the runs across the floor. Don't fret if a blemished piece gets installed. You can remove the piece or patch the gap with filler prior to finishing the floor.

Sweep the floor area and layout a row of No. 30 felt and attach it to the subfloor with staples. The felt acts as a vapor barrier and, while walking on the wood floor, will deaden the sound. Position the first row of boards on the starting line, grooved edge toward the wall. Because they are too close to the wall to use the floor nailer, the first few rows of boards will need to be face nailed. Use 8d finish nails driven below the surface with a nail set

(the hole is small and hardly noticeable after it's filled) and fill the hole.

If you install the floor with screws, drill a counterbore hole into the pieces down to the floor joist. This hole allows you to install the screw and have room left to add a plug to cover the screw head. (Plank flooring boards over $3^1/_2$"-wide should be installed with screws.)

Make a plug from matching flooring with a plug cutter and your drill or purchase plugs. Add glue to the plugs and tap them into the holes. Sand the plugs flush before finishing the floor.

Finish the row across the room, cutting the last piece to fit. If the cutoff is long enough, use it to begin the next row.

To install the second row, lay the pieces in place with the groove facing the first row. Make sure the ends are staggered, slide the piece into position and use the hammer to tap the piece tightly to the first row. To prevent damage, use a small flooring cutoff between the hammer and the piece of flooring being installed. Attach the second row to the subfloor. Fit the next piece into the first row and the end of the first piece just installed in the second row and attach it to the floor. Repeat this process for the completion of the second and third rows. After the third row is installed, you should be able to start using the floor nailer.

The Nailer Will Pick Up the Pace

Position the pieces and tap them in place. Set the nailer at the tongue-edge of the board, tighten the joint between the two boards and drive the nail through the tongue. Install nails every 16" and place a nail within 3" of each end.

If you run into a problem board — one that has a bow or is difficult to get tight to the previous board — you'll need to use the pry bar to bring them tight. This process may require you to temporarily attach a scrap to the floor to pry against. Once you get the pieces tight, drive the nails to hold it in position.

Cut and fit around obstacles in the room. For example, floor registers and wall or door openings need to be addressed.

If you come to an opening (a doorway for example) where the floor stops, turn a piece of flooring perpendicular to the main floor to create a transition piece. Locate the transition (transitioning from the wood floor level to the next level) near the middle of the doorway. If possible, allow the end tongues to fit into the transition piece. Face nail the transition piece in place.

flip tip

Installing the flooring pieces with the length-wise tongue and groove tight is important, but you need to watch the end tongue and groove as well. Fit both the end and length tongues at the same time. Tap the pieces using a mallet or hammer until the ends are tight. If tight against the wall, place the pry bar against a block of wood (not against the wall) and pry as you lightly tap on the piece. This should close the joint.

No glue is needed when installing this type of laminate flooring. The pieces are simply snapped together and you're done.

Installing Laminate Flooring

Install an underlayment of cork, foam or similar product to cushion the floor and absorb sound. Skip this step if the laminate flooring has a backing already in place. When talking with professionals, I was cautioned about pre-backed laminates. It seems there is some question about the backing failing and causing additional problems after installation. Check into this if you're looking at this type of floor.

Homeowners wishing to and willing to install their own laminate floors have three choices when purchasing laminate flooring.

First, there are traditional plank-style floors that glue together, guaranteeing a very secure bonding. The assembly and installation can be messy due to the glue. Second is pre-glued flooring — the glue is on the edges of the planks.

Swipe a damp sponge or cloth on the edge to activated the glue. As the pieces are assembled, the unit becomes a single panel that floats over the subfloor.

Third is laminate flooring (shown at left and below) assembled by locking the pieces together. There is no messy glue to work with and the pieces become a panel when snapped into position. The process of locking the pieces together varies depending on the manufacturer. Look for a thick floor because it is more likely to hold up due to a better connection. This type of floor is more costly.

Your choices depend on your budget and the time you reserve for the installation. Install the flooring designed with the locking mechanisms and you'll be walking on the finished floor as soon as you snap it in place.

**ADAMS & KENNEDY —
THE WOOD SOURCE**
6178 Mitch Owen Rd.
P.O. Box 700
Manotick, ON
Canada K4M 1A6
613-822-6803
www.wood-source.com
Wood supply

ADJUSTABLE CLAMP COMPANY
404 N. Armour St.
Chicago, IL 60622
312-666-0640
www.adjustableclamp.com
*Clamps and woodworking
tools*

B&Q
Portswood House
1 Hampshire Corporate Park
Chandlers Ford
Eastleigh
Hampshire, England
SO53 3YX
0845 609 6688
www.diy.com
*Woodworking tools, supplies
and hardware*

BUSY BEE TOOLS
130 Great Gulf Dr.
Concord, ON
Canada L4K 5W1
1-800-461-2879
www.busybeetools.com
*Woodworking tools and
supplies*

**CONSTANTINE'S WOOD CENTER
OF FLORIDA**
1040 E. Oakland Park Blvd.
Fort Lauderdale, FL 33334
800-443-9667
www.constantines.com
*Tools, woods, veneers,
hardware*

**FRANK PAXTON LUMBER
COMPANY**
5701 W. 66th St.
Chicago, IL 60638
800-323-2203
www.paxtonwood.com
Wood, hardware, tools, books

THE HOME DEPOT
2455 Paces Ferry Rd. NW
Atlanta, GA 30339
800-553-3376 (U.S.)
800-628-0525 (Canada)
www.homedepot.com
*Woodworking tools, supplies
and hardware*

KLINGSPOR ABRASIVES INC.
800-645-5555
www.klingspor.com
Sandpaper of all kinds

LEE VALLEY TOOLS LTD.
P.O. Box 1780
Ogdensburg, NY 13669-6780
800-871-8158 (U.S.)
800-267-8767 (Canada)
www.leevalley.com
*Woodworking tools and
hardware*

LOWE'S COMPANIES, INC.
P.O. Box 1111
North Wilkesboro, NC 28656
800-445-6937
www.lowes.com
*Woodworking tools, supplies
and hardware*

**ROCKLER WOODWORKING
AND HARDWARE**
4365 Willow Dr.
Medina, MN 55340
800-279-4441
www.rockler.com
*Woodworking tools,
hardware and books*

**TREND MACHINERY & CUTTING
TOOLS LTD.**
Odhams Trading Estate
St. Albans Rd.
Watford
Hertfordshire, U.K.
WD24 7TR
01923 224657
www.trendmachinery.co.uk
*Woodworking tools and
hardware*

WATERLOX COATINGS
908 Meech Ave.
Cleveland, OH 44105
800-321-0377
www.waterlox.com
Finishing supplies

WOODCRAFT SUPPLY LLC
1177 Rosemar Rd.
P.O. Box 1686
Parkersburg, WV 26102
800-535-4482
www.woodcraft.com
Woodworking hardware

WOODWORKER'S HARDWARE
P.O. Box 180
Sauk Rapids, MN 56379-0180
800-383-0130
www.wwhardware.com
Woodworking hardware

WOODWORKER'S SUPPLY
1108 N. Glenn Rd.
Casper, WY 82601
800-645-9292
http://woodworker.com
*Woodworking tools and
accessories, finishing
supplies, books and plans*

index

MORE GREAT TITLES FROM F+W PUBLICATIONS!

MEASURE TWICE, CUT ONCE
By Jim Tolpin

From design and layout to developing a cutting list, Jim Tolpin's easy-to-follow style introduces a variety of tools (new and old) used to transfer measurements accurately to the wood. You'll learn the best cutting techniques, how to prevent mistakes before they happen, and for those unavoidable mistakes, you'll learn how to fix them so no one will know!

ISBN 13: 978-1-55870-809-9
ISBN 10: 1-55870-809-X
paperback, 128 p., #Z0835

THE COMPLETE CUSTOM CLOSET
By Chris Gleason

How would you like to create a storage or work area that isn't just a black hole behind some doors? You can make your closets what they should be — organized, orderly and well-utilized spaces. With step-by-step photos, captions, sidebars and tips, this book shows you how you can create your own custom closets quickly and easily.

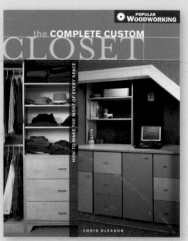

ISBN 13: 978-1-55870-777-1
ISBN 10: 1-55870-777-8
paperback, 128 p., # Z0027

I CAN DO THAT! WOODWORKING PROJECTS
Edited by David Thiel

Beginning or experienced woodworkers can build these top-quality projects quickly and efficiently.
- Each project requires a minimum of tools
- The projects need only inexpensive materials that are readily available at your local home improvement center
- This book includes a training manual for using each tool

ISBN 13: 978-1-55870-816-7
ISBN 10: 1-55870-816-2
paperback, 128 p., #Z0991

WOODSHOP STORAGE SOLUTIONS
By Ralph Laughton

Are you constantly looking for better and more efficient ways of storing and using your tools? This book contains 16 ingenious projects that will make your woodshop totally efficient, extremely flexible and very safe. Projects include: down-draft table, clamp rack, mobile table-saw stand, router trolley, router table and more.

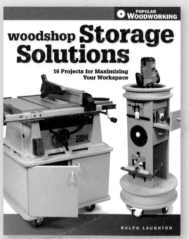

ISBN 13: 978-1-55870-784-9
ISBN 10: 1-55870-784-0
paperback, 128 p., # Z0348

These and other great woodworking books are available at your local bookstore, woodworking stores or from online suppliers.

www.popularwoodworking.com